Mastermind Two

D0544994

Mastermind Two

questions and answers from the BBC tv quiz game
compiled by Boswell Taylor

British Broadcasting Corporation

Published by the British Broadcasting Corporation,
35 Marylebone High Street, London W1M 4AA

ISBN 0 563 12866 6

First published 1975

© Boswell Taylor 1975

Printed in England by Hunt Barnard Printing Ltd,
Aylesbury, Bucks

The General Knowledge questions have been selected
from those submitted to the programme by
Ann Allen and John Witty

Contents

General Knowledge 1

1 On what day of the Creation did God make the Sun, Moon and stars?

2 Lollius Urbicus was responsible for building a defensive wall against Scottish tribes. What was it called?

3 Edda is the name given to two important collections of literature, of which country?

4 Who commanded the Indian forces at Little Big Horn?

5 In Greek mythology anemones sprang from his blood after he had been gored by a wild boar. Who was he?

6 Where was the first World Cup held?

7 Timbuktu was founded in 1807. Whereabouts is it?

8 What are blue brindles, headers, flettons, and common reds?

9 Which war was brought to an end by the surrender of forces under the command of General Cornwallis?

10 Mr Russell Means led a group of people in revolt against Government. Who were they?

11 He negotiated the Louisiana Purchase in 1803, and in 1816 was elected fifth President of the USA. Who was he?

12 Dicentra Spectabilis is a plant. By what other name is it known?

13 Which modern author would you associate with Glencoe, Culloden and the Highland Clearances?

14 Who is supposed to have established the measurement of a yard?

15 Who was immortalised in George Borrow's novels *Lavengro* and *Romany Rye*?

16 In medieval times what was the Mangonel used for?

17 Who are designated by the term Scotists?

18 How many records are castaways allowed to take to their imaginary island in 'Desert Island Discs'?

19 Tisiphone, Magaera and Alecto pursued earthly sinners. Who were they?

20 Who described assassination as 'the extreme form of censorship'?

Astronomy

Set by Patrick Moore

21 Which planet has a Great Red Spot?

22 What is remarkable about the direction of a comet's tail?

23 What kind of variable star is Algol?

24 In which lunar sea did the Apollo 11 astronauts land in 1969?

25 Who first suggested the principle of the reflecting telescope?

26 Which two planets in the Solar System show lunar-type phases as seen from Earth?

27 Which is the more distant – a pulsar or a quasar?

28 Which spacecraft sent back the first close-range pictures of Venus?

29 Which is the brightest of the asteroids?

30 Which bright periodical comet will return to perihelion in 1986?

31 What is meant by saying that the Moon is at syzygy?

32 What is the name of the bright meteor shower seen every August?

33 What is the colour of an F-type star?

34 Which is the only satellite in the Solar System known to have a reasonably dense atmosphere?

35 In which lunar 'sea' would you find the crater Bessel?

36 Where would you find the Nix Olympica and the Syrtis Major?

37 What famous celestial object is known officially as Messier 31?

38 Who was the Danish astronomer who measured the velocity of light in 1675?

39 Which major planet was discovered in 1846?

40 Where, today, would you find the crater named after Dr Gerard P. Kuiper?

PATRICK MOORE: Well-known television personality, author, and expert on astronomy.

Legends of Britain

Set by T. A. Shippey

41 First in the line of kings that includes Cymbeline, old King Cole and King Arthur, who was this legendary founder of Britain?

42 From which city did Brutus originate?

43 Whose is the 'Isle of Gramarye' quoted by T. H. White in the opening verse to *The Once and Future King*?

44 Which Welsh king is said to have invited Hengest and Horsa into Britain?

45 In Burns's *Tam o' Shanter*, the hero used a legendary method of escaping from witches. What was this?

46 Who is said to have rescued England from the Danes by killing their giant Colbrand?

47 In his legendary exploits, what abbey was sacked by Hereward the Wake?

48 What is a silkie?

49 Which saint nipped the Devil's nose with red-hot tongs?

50 Who was the legendary foster-son of Grim of Grimsby?

51 According to the Tudor dramatists, and William Stukeley's pedigree, of which county was Robin Hood the rightful earl?

52 Who made the 'brazen head' at Oxford?

53 What is a kelpie?

54 Peg Powler appears in Teesside legends and Jenny Greenteeth in Lancashire legends. What were they?

55 In the Welsh *Mabinogi*, who was 'Prince of Dyfed', called 'Pen Annwn', the 'Head of Hades', and who reigned at Narberth?

56 According to Briggs' *Dictionary of Folk Lore*, which race knew the secret of the 'heather ale'?

57 In which British county is Pontius Pilate said to be born, with a yew to mark his birthplace?

58 What did young Lambton catch when fishing in the Wear?

59 At what time of year is the Glastonbury thorn said to flower?

60 Who brought the Holy Grail from Palestine to England?

T. A. SHIPPEY, M.A.: St John's College, Oxford.

General Knowledge 2

61 Who was the goddess who mooned about Endymion?

62 What substance was responsible for the phrase 'mad as a Hatter'?

63 Which famous English novelist collaborated on the libretto of *Billy Budd* (Benjamin Britten's opera)?

64 What solo instrument is featured in the Largo of Dvořák's *New World* Symphony?

65 What was the official residence of British sovereigns from 1698 until 1837?

66 What is the name of the earliest known Chinese Dynasty?

67 Who was Britain's second-in-command at the Battle of Copenhagen in 1801?

68 'Court' cards on British packs are costumed as of the time of which monarch?

69 Who was the French artist who painted *The Progress of Love* for Madame du Barry?

70 What does the abbreviation O.L.A.S. stand for?

71 What Victorian novelist adopted the pseudonym Michael Angelo Titmarsh?

72 What should you be brought in a restaurant if you order Bigorneaux?

73 What was the name popularly given to women who sat knitting by the guillotine?

74 Who is the Peruvian who once won the Wimbledon Singles Lawn Tennis Championships?

75 What is myosotis better known as?

76 How many hoops are used in a game of croquet?

77 Noël Coward's play *Still Life* was adapted as a film. What was it then called?

78 Where in London exactly is the Mermaid Theatre sited?

79 Who directed the classic Russian film *Battleship Potemkin*?

80 In 1958 the French established the Fifth Republic, which was approved by all French territories except one. Which one?

20th-Century British Politics

Set by Dr David Butler

81   What was the shortest premiership in this century?

82   What was the Liberal Party's first post-war
     by-election win?

83   How long was David Lloyd George a Minister?

84   When did women get the vote at 21?

85   Who was the first Secretary of State for Wales?

86   Who was the first Scottish National Party MP?

87   Give the years for the two Nationalisations of steel.

88   Who finally took Britain off the gold standard?

89   Which was the first general election in which public
     opinion polls were published?

90   How many times did Winston Churchill stand for
     Parliament unsuccessfully?

91   Who established the Cabinet Secretariat?

92   Who announced the first 'Wage Freeze'?

93   What was the dramatic affair at Invergordon in 1931?

94   What was the official position of Sir Warren Fisher
     from 1919 to 1939?

95   Who was the first Minister of Munitions?

96   Under whose premiership were Life Peerages
     introduced?

97 What have Bewdley, Warwick and Leamington, and Bexley in common?

98 When were MPs first paid?

99 What was the Taff Vale decision?

100 Who were the hedgers and who were the ditchers?

DR DAVID E. BUTLER, M.A., D.Phil.: Fellow of Nuffield College, Oxford. Author of: *The British General Election of 1951, The Electoral System in Britain 1918–1951, The British General Election of 1955, British Political Facts 1900–1966*, etc.

Science Fiction

Set by T. A. Shippey

101 What did Winston Smith find in room 101?

102 In Gordon Dickson's stories, what does the world of 'the Dorsai' export?

103 Complete this sentence: 'Space is a province of —'

104 What letter should precede the name Daneel Olivaw?

105 Teela Brown was selected to explore the Ringworld for one quality. What was it?

106 In which book are these creatures to be found: crocksocks, traversers, burnurns, killerwillows?

107 In which story are these creatures implements of war: Termagants, Juggers, Fiends, Blue Horrors?

108 Which author created the concept of 'slow glass'?

109 In which book would you find Captain Washington working with Sir Isambard Brunel?

110 In which book would you find a Mickey Mouse watch regarded as an *objet d'art*?

111 For what was Delos D. Harriman famous?

112 What was the name of E. E. Smith's 'Gray Lensman'?

113 For what was the Blessed Leibowitz martyred?

114 Of which classic short story are these the last few words: 'Robot atom bombs do not make up their own minds'?

115 Which author created doctor Calhoun and his *tormal* Murgatroyd?

116 Which planet is defended by 'Mother Hitton's Littul Kittons'?

117 The first Earthman to visit the stars travelled inside a sperm whale: in which book?

118 The philosopher Bokonon informs us that a *granfalloon* is a false *karass*: in which book?

119 In Kipling's story 'As Easy as A.B.C.', what does A.B.C. stand for?

120 Why was Barlennan the Mesklinite afraid of heights?

T. A. SHIPPEY, M.A.: St John's College, Oxford.

General Knowledge 3

121 Mohorovičić Discontinuity describes what?

122 What was the special happening at Massabielle, on the banks of the River Gave, 115 years ago?

123 Who was the first Negro to be awarded the Nobel Peace Prize?

124 Which German pocket battleship in 1939 was out-manoeuvred to such an extent by three British cruisers that her Commander was forced to scuttle her?

125 On what story is the musical *Chu Chin Chow* based?

126 In what sort of building is a working area called the 'prompt side'?

127 Who is the English novelist who has made a speciality of one word titles, such as *Loving*, *Living*, *Caught* and *Nothing*?

128 How long is an American Presidential term?

129 Of what nationality was the physicist Ohm?

130 Who was responsible for giving us 'Bank Holidays'?

131 The standard language of China is based on the Chinese of Peking. What is its name?

132 What is the modern Turkish name for the mound where the city of Troy stood?

133 What was surrendered to Lieutenant-General Tomoyuki Yamashita on 15 February 1942?

134 Where would you find the piece of ordnance known as 'Mons Meg'?

135 In 1572 who observed a nova in the constellation of Cassiopeia?

136 Which highly developed civilisation preceded the Aztecs in Mexico?

137 Why was Julian called the Apostate?

138 What term is used to express 1/10th of a nautical mile?

139 Who was the ancient Egyptian God of the Sun?

140 What is the correct name for the upper body shell of tortoises and crustaceans?

Gilbert and Sullivan

Set by Albert Truelove

141. What was the name of the girl whom the Judge married in *Trial by Jury*?

142. Name four of the items of food the villagers had for tea in *The Sorcerer*.

143. Which portrait comes alive in *Ruddigore* and marries an old flame who has survived him? And what is the name of the old flame?

144. What movements does Gilbert satirise in (a) *Trial by Jury*, (b) *Patience*, (c) *Princess Ida*?

145. What is the first line of the song first used in *Thespis* and then repeated in *The Pirates of Penzance*?

146. Which are the two places in London where hearts may beat as pure and fair?

147. Whom did Elsie marry in *The Yeomen of the Guard*, and how much was she paid?

148. If Colonel Fairfax had not married, what was the name of the character who would have succeeded to his estate?

149. In *The Gondoliers* there are two gondoliers, Marco and Giuseppe. What are the names of their respective brides?

150. Although the Savoy Theatre is associated with Gilbert and Sullivan operas, what was the name of the other London theatre opened by Richard D'Oyly Carte, and what was the name of the grand opera written by Sullivan that opened it?

151. What was the name of the first Gilbert and Sullivan opera?

152 When Katisha denies that she is beautiful, what is it that she has that she says is a miracle of loveliness?

153 Name three of the crimes committed by Sir Ruthven Murgatroyd.

154 Why didn't Sir Ruthven Murgatroyd commit a crime on Monday?

155 Name King Gama's three sons in *Princess Ida*.

156 What relations did Sir Joseph Porter bring on board 'H.M.S. Pinafore' with him?

157 What advice does Sir Joseph Porter give in order to become the ruler of the Queen's Navy?

158 At which theatre was *The Pirates of Penzance* performed in order to obtain the British copyright?

159 Where did the London première of *The Pirates of Penzance* take place and when?

160 Who was in the audience at the first night of *Iolanthe* who suddenly found himself being sung to by name?

ALBERT TRUELOVE: Secretary, Bridget D'Oyly Carte Ltd.

Greek Mythology
Set by Dr Wolfgang Liebeschuetz

161   What bird was associated with the goddess Athena?

162   How did Achilles die?

163   When Odysseus returned home he was recognised by his old dog. Name the dog.

164   A divine husband caught his wife in bed with the god of war and entangled both in a net as a laughing stock for the gods. Who was the husband?

165   How did Apollo punish Cassandra for refusing his love?

166   On returning home from Troy Agamemnon was killed by his wife, Clytemnestra, and her lover. Name the lover.

167   A King tried to stop the worship of Dionysus and was torn to pieces by his mother. Who was he?

168   A Greek god with horns, beard, tail and goat's feet lived in wild places and enjoyed frightening travellers. Name him.

169   With what princess did Zeus unite in the shape of a rain of gold?

170   The British Museum has famous carvings of Centaurs fighting Lapiths. Why did they fight?

171   Who was the mother of Hercules?

172   How many sons did Priam have by Hecuba?

173   Which Athenian princess was saved from the wrath of her brother-in-law by being transformed into a nightingale?

174 Why did the *curetes* clash their weapons around the infant Zeus?

175 Homer contains a single reference to a message in writing. Who carried it?

176 What god roared like a bull after being wounded by a Greek hero at Troy?

177 Who were the parents of the Minotaur?

178 'O for a beaker full of the warm south,
Full of the true, the blushful Hippocrene.'
(Keats, 'Ode to a Nightingale') What was the original 'Hippocrene'?

179 A Mycenean settlement has been preserved by a thick layer of volcanic ashes. Where?

180 The goddess Demeter acted as nurse to an infant prince. The locality became the scene of a famous initiation festival. What was its name?

DR WOLFGANG LIEBESCHUETZ: Department of Classics, Leicester University.

General Knowledge 4

181   Who, in politics, were the Adullamites?

182   In the canine sense, what is the etymology of the word 'terrier'?

183   The hero of a Babylonian epic offended the goddess Ishtar and was punished. How was he punished?

184   Who was the sculptor of Lord Nelson's statue in Trafalgar Square?

185   The site of one of the seven wonders of the ancient world was discovered in the nineteenth century. Which one?

186   In which book would you expect to find Piscator – a fisherman, Auceps – a fowler, Venator – a hunter?

187   Which country declared itself an independent republic on 17 June 1944?

188   What is the Japanese word for 'Good-bye'?

189   In which famous book would you find the characters Denisov and Dolokhov?

190   In what year did Marx and Engels issue the Communist Manifesto?

191   In classical legend, who were the Moirae?

192   Name the four breeds of draught horses used in the United Kingdom.

193   Of which country did Sir Seretse Khama become President?

194   Alice Liddell received a Christmas gift in memory of a summer's day. What was it?

195 From what fruit was marmalade originally made?

196 What substance is processed in a Ginnery?

197 In which novel would you find reference to the 'Black Riders' and 'Cracks of Doom'?

198 What is the name of the vestment worn by deacons over their left shoulders?

199 What part of a horse-drawn carriage is a Felloe or Felly?

200 Who wrote *The Cabinet-Maker and Upholsterer's Guide*?

British Ornithology

Set by Bruce Campbell

201 What are the popular names for the bony structure called the furcula?

202 Where is the alula?

203 What is an eclipse plumage?

204 Which British bird has most feathers?

205 What is the gonys and what is its purpose?

206 What is a nidifugous species?

207 How would you distinguish an adult female great spotted woodpecker *Dendrocopos major* from an adult male in the field?

208 What is the most favoured winter food of the bullfinch *Pyrrhula pyrrhula*?

209 Why is a male falcon called a tiercel?

210 *Caprimulgus*: to what bird does this name refer and why?

211 Two Kentish place names occur in the common names of British birds (not counting the Kentish plover *Charadruis alexandrinus*); what are they?

212 What, ornithologically, have Sula Sgeir, North Rona, St Kilda and Flannan Isles in common?

213 Three-quarters of the world breeding population of a sea bird is concentrated round the British Isles: which species?

214 To what is the remarkable spread of the fulmar petrel
     Fulmarus glacialis round the British Isles usually
     attributed?

215 With what rare breeding bird do you particularly
     associate Minsmere and Havergate Island
     in Suffolk?

216 What notable event in British ornithology took place
     on the island of Fetlar (Shetland)?

217 When did the golden eagle *Aquila chrysaetos* last
     nest in England?

218 What bird is recorded as nesting on a Scottish
     Cathedral in 1416?

219 What flightless bird was found in Britain in
     historic times?

220 Which is the smallest British bird?

DR BRUCE CAMPBELL: Joint Honorary Secretary, Council for
Nature; Council Member, the Wildfowl Trust; Member,
Scientific Advisory Committee, Royal Society for the
Protection of Birds.

United States Presidents

Set by Professor D. K. Adams

221 How many times was Franklin D. Roosevelt elected president?

222 What is the address of the White House?

223 Who assassinated President Garfield and where did it happen?

224 Whose ambition was said to be 'a little engine that knew no rest'?

225 Which President was known as 'the little Magician'?

226 Name the university of which Dwight D. Eisenhower was president in the late 1940s.

227 Who said, and on what occasion: 'Against the insidious wiles of foreign influence . . . the jealousy of a free people ought to be *constantly* awake'?

228 To which political party did Rutherford B. Hayes belong?

229 What was the family relationship of Presidents William Henry Harrison and Benjamin Harrison?

230 Who was the first US president to be awarded the Nobel Peace Prize and for what was it awarded?

231 Whose portrait is on the $5 bill?

232 Who was the only bachelor president?

233 According to Article II(2) of the Constitution, who, after the vice-president, is next in line for the presidency?

234 Who lived at 'The Hermitage'?

235 Which former president later became Chief Justice of the US Supreme Court?

236 In which city did the inauguration of John Adams take place?

237 Who was the author of *The Winning of the West*?

238 Who succeeded President Tyler?

239 According to the Constitution, what is the minimum age that a president has to be?

240 Who first planted poplars along Pennsylvania Avenue to beautify the city of Washington?

PROFESSOR D. K. ADAMS, M.A., D.Phil: Department of American Studies, Keele University.

General Knowledge 5

241 For what are the Caves of Lascaux famous?

242 Who was Escoffier?

243 What is the mathematical term that means without
     end or limit?

244 Chequers is the official country residence of the
     Prime Minister. Where is it?

245 Which country has borders with Austria,
     Czechoslavakia, Russia, Romania, and
     Yugoslavia?

246 Which game originated in Persia, but takes its name
     from the Tibetan for ball? It was introduced into
     England in 1869.

247 Who said: 'The philosophers have only interpreted
     the world, in various ways; the point, however, is
     to change it'?

248 Jaroslav Hasek wrote a novel about a soldier.
     What was it called?

249 Of which islands is Hugh Town the capital?

250 According to Greek mythology whom did Apollo's
     lyre come from?

251 The General Strike in 1926 was called in support
     of which union?

252 The term 'Impressionism' was first used abusively to
     describe which artist's painting of a sunrise?

253 In 1519 the *Trinidad*, *San Antonio*, *Concepcion*, *Vittoria* and *Santiago* made up the fleet of a famous explorer. Who was he?

254 Indonesia was declared a Republic in 1945. Who was its first President?

255 From which of Burns's poems are these lines taken:
      'I am truly sorry man's dominion
        Has broken nature's social union'?

256 The Germans call this World War I battle the Battle of the Skagerrak. By what other name is it know?

257 Japanese have two popular forms of wrestling. Judo is one, what is the other?

258 Who was the Swedish Nightingale?

259 In a Parliamentary Election, what percentage of votes does a candidate need to avoid losing his deposit?

260 What is the supreme policy-making body of the Soviet Union?

The Works of J. R. R. Tolkien

Set by T. A. Shippey

261 How many rings 'for the dwarf-lords in their halls of stone'?

262 What was the nickname of Thorin son of Thráin son of Thror?

263 What was the nickname of Gríma (pronounced Greema) son of Gálmód (Garl-mode)?

264 What was the name given to Saruman in the Shire?

265 Who killed the dragon Smaug?

266 For what was Tobold Hornblower of Longbottom in the Southfarthing famous?

267 What shape could Beorn the skin-changer take besides the human one?

268 What was the name of Gandalf's sword?

269 What was Gollum's original name?

270 What was the name of the inn kept by Barliman Butterbur?

271 Which river ran through the Old Forest?

272 Who was the master of the Last Homely House east of the Sea?

273 In the Shire Calendar, what is the month between Winterfilth and Foreyule?

274 Who was given the advice 'Seek for the Sword that was broken'?

275 What did Galadriel (pronounced Ga*lad*riel) give to Sam Gamgee (Gam-jee)?

276 Of which race were trolls made in mockery?

277 What is the common or rustic term for the herb 'athelas'?

278 Whose epitaph begins 'Faithful servant yet master's bane'?

279 What was the device on the King of Rohan's flag? (pronounced Roe-han)

280 What is the supposed etymology of the word 'hobbit'?

T. A. SHIPPEY, M.A.: St John's College, Oxford.

Grand Opera since Verdi

Set by Harold Rosenthal

281   On what poem is Britten's *Peter Grimes* based?

282   What was unique about the first performance of Puccini's *Turandot* at La Scala, Milan, in 1926?

283   What opera by Richard Strauss is autobiographical?

284   What was the last opera performed at the Vienna State Opera before it was destroyed by bombs in World War II?

285   In opera, who was the 'Young Lord'?

286   Who walked to the Paradise Garden?

287   Which opera has been dubbed the poor man's *Traviata*?

288   Who were the librettists of Stravinsky's *Rake's Progress*?

289   What was the first Jazz opera?

290   What does Strauss introduce anachronistically into *Der Rosenkavalier*?

291   Who was the master-jeweller who murdered his victims rather than part with the creations he had made for them?

292   Who was the King of Allemonde?

293   Which opera singer lived for 300 years?

294   What was the sequel that Charpentier wrote to his *Louise*?

295 On what dramas is Berg's *Lulu* based?

296 What opera tells of the martyrdom of members of a religious order during the French Revolution?

297 Why was Strauss's *Schweigsame Frau* banned by the Nazis after only three performances?

298 Which was the first opera that made use of the quarter-tone scale?

299 On what quotation is Strauss's *Capriccio* based?

300 What opera lead to the formulation of 'socialist realism' as an artistic principle in the USSR?

HAROLD ROSENTHAL: Editor of *Opera*.

General Knowledge 6

301 The Chiltern Hundreds consist of three stewardships. Stoke and Burnham are two, what is the third?

302 A bathroom scale is a simple type of computer. What type?

303 Which philosopher coined the phrase, 'Cogito ergo sum'?

304 Who was the last king of Israel – he ruled from 732 to 724 BC?

305 Which Saint translated the Vulgate?

306 Doctor George MacLeod founded a religious community. What is it called?

307 In which city did Harold Macmillan make his 'wind of change' speech?

308 What is the name of the famous whirlpool between the islands of Moskenesøya and Vaerøy?

309 Can you say what vodka really means?

310 What is the name of the special straw used to drink maté or Paraguay Tea?

311 What sort of person is a benedick?

312 Who wrote the mid-Victorian novels of 'Barsetshire'?

313 What American state is nicknamed 'Show Me State'?

314 What is Caper-spurge?

315 Which European prince was called 'The Navigator'?

316 What befell Arachne when she challenged Athena at weaving?

317 Who wrote under the occasional pen-name of 'Peter Porcupine'?

318 Who designed the Welsh town of Portmeirion?

319 To what islands was Archbishop Makarios exiled (in 1956)?

320 Upon whose work was the Julian calendar based?

The Old Testament

Set by Professor A. R. C. Leaney

321 In the Garden of Eden story, what were Adam and Eve forbidden to eat?

322 What plague brought upon Egypt moved the magicians to say: 'This is the finger of God'?

323 In what place did the Lord first appear to Moses?

324 What was the name of the army officer with whose wife David committed adultery?

325 When David died who contended with Solomon for the throne?

326 In the book of Esther who was the queen whose place was taken by Esther?

327 Which king consulted the witch (or 'woman that hath a familiar spirit') at Endor?

328 From what village did the prophet Jeremiah come?

329 What decorative material is associated with the house built by Ahab for himself?

330 Naaman the Syrian came to Elisha to be cured of leprosy; what did Elisha prescribe?

331 What was the name of the last king of Judah in the Old Testament?

332 Name the three friends who came to talk to Job in his misery.

333 Where can be found the prophecy that men would turn their spears into pruning-hooks?

334 With what subject is the book of Nahum occupied?

335 What name did the prophet Hosea give to the daughter born to him by his wife Gomer?

336 What was the historical occasion of Isaiah's prophecy which begins with the words: 'A young woman is with child, and she will bear a son, and will call him Immanuel' (Isaiah 7.14)?

337 When did the prophet Haggai prophesy?

338 What was the disaster which moved the prophet Joel to call for a national fast?

339 Job chapter 28 is a poem on the search for Wisdom. How does it end?

340 'The Lord' is a substitute for the name of God as revealed to Moses. What consonants represent the actual Hebrew name?

PROFESSOR A. R. C. LEANEY, MA, DD: formerly Department of Theology, University of Nottingham.

The New Testament

Set by Professor A. R. C. Leaney

341 In the Gospel of Mark what are the first few words uttered by Jesus?

342 In the Gospel of John, who were the first two disciples to join Jesus?

343 In the story of the Temptations of Jesus, from what book of the Old Testament does he answer the devil?

344 Name the parents of John the Baptist.

345 Give the two different names of the disciple called from the 'receipt of custom'.

346 At what point in the story did Mary say the Magnificat?

347 Name the co-author with Paul of I Corinthians.

348 Where did the visions recorded in the book of Revelation take place?

349 What was the name of the scribe to whom Paul dictated his letter to the Romans?

350 Which was the first town in Europe evangelised by Paul?

351 In what books of the New Testament does the word Antichrist occur?

352 What are the two Aramaic words recorded in the Gospel of Mark as spoken by Jesus to a twelve-year-old girl, and what do they mean?

353 To whom is the Letter of James addressed?

354 When Paul and Barnabas split up, where did Barnabas go?

355 What festival was it when 'On the last . . . day of the Festival Jesus . . . cried "If anyone is thirsty, let him come to me" '?

356 To whom was the letter addressed from the Council at Jerusalem described in Acts 15?

357 What passage in the New Testament appears to support the tradition that Mark was a follower of Peter?

358 What clues are given in Acts as to the date when Paul was first in Corinth?

359 What action of Paul's at Lystra apparently contradicts his teaching that the authority of the Law had been destroyed by Christ?

360 How many visits did Paul pay to Corinth (a) according to Acts (b) according to the evidence of his letters?

PROFESSOR A. R. C. LEANEY, MA, DD: formerly Department of Theology, University of Nottingham.

General Knowledge 7

361 In what type of space capsule did John Glen first circle the earth?

362 It was owned by the Barberini family until 1780, smashed by a maniac in 1845, repaired and is now owned by the nation. What is it?

363 In which city would you find the Jacques Cartier Bridge?

364 *Pulex irritans* is a parasitic insect. What is it more commonly known as?

365 Osborne Henry Mavor was a Scottish author. Under what pseudonym did he write?

366 At the time of Edward VIII's abdication, who was Prime Minister?

367 As an expert in excavating and tunnelling, this Australian animal stands supreme. What is it called?

368 What did the Polish corridor give to Poland after the first World War?

369 'The better part of valour is discretion.' Who said this?

370 If you lapidated someone, what would you be doing to them?

371 What 20th-century war did the Treaty of Portsmouth end?

372 In astronomy, what is an Occultation?

373 What is the name of the Moorish palace in Granada which is named after the Arabic word for *the red*?

374 Of whom was it said: 'He will be looked upon by posterity as a brave, bad man'?

375 Across which city does the statue of Christ on the Corcovado look?

376 Which battle in 1882 marked the beginning of British occupation in Egypt?

377 The Royal Standard is divided into quarters. The first and fourth contain three lions passant, the second the lion rampant, what is the third?

378 She became famous with her writings on proper behaviour and good manners. One of her books was entitled *Etiquette*. Who was she?

379 Describe the European flag.

380 What was the original name for the Royal Albert Hall?

The Works of Dorothy L. Sayers

Set by Julian Symons

381 What is the motto of the Wimsey family?

382 Give the full name of the man who wrote a short
biography of Lord Peter Wimsey.

383 What were Lord Peter's clubs, as mentioned in his
Who's Who entry?

384 In one book Dorothy Sayers had a collaborator.
What was his name?

385 What was the name of Harriet Vane's chief
defence counsel?

386 What was Sir Impey's hobby?

387 Who gave away Harriet Vane at her marriage?

388 What happened to the Warden immediately after
the marriage?

389 According to Bunter's letter to his wife, how long
had he been in Lord Peter's service at the time
of the marriage?

390 At the marriage, what was the bride's gift to the
groom?

391 Who capped a Wordsworth quotation of Lord
Peter's by another from the same poet?

392 'Tell Bunter to give you a bottle of the . . . , it's rather
decent,' Lord Peter says to Parker. What was
the wine?

393 Where did Lord Peter and Miss Tarrant go to dinner?

394 What was the address of Lord Peter's bachelor flat?

395 Lord Peter called it 'The case of cases, the murder without discernible means, or motive, or clue'. What book gives an account of it?

396 To what murderer does Lord Peter say that he's a decent fellow, and that 'in your place I know what I should do'?

397 What was the subject of Miss Lydgate's forthcoming work?

398 What happened to the manuscript introduction to the work, which she lent to Harriet Vane?

399 Who is written to as 'Darling Old Bungie, old thing', in what book?

400 How did Dr Waters describe the cause of a case of muscarine poisoning?

JULIAN SYMONS: Well-known critic and detective novelist; author of *The Detective Novel*.

Norse Mythology

Set by Professor Peter G. Foote

401 What is the name of Thor's hammer?

402 Which god was born of nine mothers?

403 Who was the blind god, and for what is he chiefly famous?

404 Which goddess owned the necklace called Brisinga-men?

405 What weapon did Freyr use against the giant Beli (Bell-i)?

406 Which tree is called the 'salvation of Thor'?

407 What was Draupnir and what its peculiar virtue?

408 Why does one associate the number eight with Sleipnir (Slaypneer) and Starkath (or Starkather)?

409 For what benefits did people invoke the god Njorth(ur) (Nyorth(er))?

410 What was made of the blood of Kvasir mixed with honey?

411 What was Naglfar (Naggle-far) supposed to be made of, and who steers it at the Doom of the Gods?

412 What did Thor do to the dwarf Lit(ur) (Litt(er)) after Baldur's death?

413 Who was called the 'god of hanged men' and why?

414 How did Loki (Lokki) rescue Ithunn and her apples from the giants?

415 Thokk (or perhaps Loki in disguise) said: 'Let Hel keep what she has' – what did Hel have?

416 Why could a poet call a shield 'the seat of the soles of Hrungnir's feet'?

417 What did Othin first gain from his self-immolation?

418 In early poetry Hlin (Hleen) appears as a name of Frigg. Who does Snorri say Hlin was?

419 What is the main difference between Baldur in Snorri's Edda and Balderus in Saxo's Gesta Danorum?

420 We are told a heathen oath was: 'So help me Njorth(ur) (Nyorth(er)) and Freyr and the almighty one of the AEsir (Ayseer)'. Why do some scholars think this contains evidence of Christian influence?

PROFESSOR PETER FOOTE: Professor of Old Scandinavian and Director of Scandinavian Studies, University College London. Secretary, Viking Society, Chevalier, Icelandic Order of the Falcon. Author: *The Viking Achievement*, etc.

General Knowledge 8

421 Whom did Jenny von Westphalen marry?

422 Which French town housed the British Army Headquarters between 1914 and 1916?

423 Kipling wrote: 'Let us admit it fairly, as a business people should, we have had no end of a lesson'. What was the lesson?

424 In Greek legend King Minos of Crete demanded yearly payment. What was this payment?

425 What are the Latin words often used to express the meanings: (a) word for word (b) letter for letter?

426 How many operas comprise the Ring Cycle?

427 He was a French astrologer, consulted among others by Catherine de'Medici. Who was he?

428 In Roman myth, who opened the gates of heaven every morning for the Sun God Apollo?

429 Who was the designer of the airship R 100?

430 In the history of New Orleans in America three flags have flown over the city on different occasions. Of what nationalities were they?

431 Who, according to legend, was the second wife of Priam and mother of Hector, Paris and Cassandra, among others?

432 Who led the Chetniks in their war-time Resistance movement?

433 The Egyptian god Anubis had the head of an animal. Which animal?

434 He developed his own theory of analytical psychology, and wrote *Modern Man in Search of a Soul*. Who was he?

435 By whom was Erithacus rubecula murdered?

436 A horse's height is measured from the ground – to what point?

437 For what kind of art is Roy Lichtenstein famous?

438 Who was the only British king of the House of Saxe-Coburg?

439 'The eternal mystery of the world is its comprehensibility.' Who said this?

440 Cesare Borgia was the favourite son of his father. Who was his father?

Railways of Great Britain

Set by Ian Allan

441   What is the wheel arrangement of a 'Mikado'-type locomotive?

442   Until recently there were four terminal stations in Glasgow. What were they?

443   Which was the *number* of the last steam locomotive to be built by BR?

444   The locomotive 'King George' is still operating. What was its BR running number?

445   Another GWR locomotive named 'Lloyds' had an unusual number. What was it?

446   What is the longest station platform in Great Britain?

447   What is the function of a short-armed signal with horizontal red, white and red stripes surmounted by the letter 'C'?

448   On what voltage does the London Midland Southport electric service operate?

449   What does the term 'Syphon G' mean to you?

450   Two lines which might be termed 'Underground' railways are operated by BR. What are they?

451   The former 'Southern Electric' system was developed under a famous General Manager. Who?

452   There was once a regular through service from Windsor to Victoria. What route did it take?

453   BR operate several shipping services but only one is inland. Where does it operate from?

454 What is the horse power of a Class AL5 electric locomotive?

455 Pontypridd used to be an important junction on the former GWR but what was the original owning Company?

456 What is an 'RKB'?

457 A specific locomotive was allocated to haul Southern Railway's royal trains. What was its number and class?

458 Midland Railway operated a mineral line from Whatstandwell, trains being hauled for part of their journey by cable. What was it called?

459 At which station in Birmingham do express trains from Paddington arrive?

460 What is the most northerly station on BR?

IAN ALLAN: Publisher of magazines and books on railways and other transport subjects.

British Chemical Industry

Set by Dr T. F. West

461 Which party leader has worked as a research chemist in industry?

462 Which class of compounds are polymers (e.g. polyethylene) made from?

463 What is the main use of an alkyl benzene sulphonate?

464 Which two companies, besides BP and Esso, produce ethylene in the UK?

465 At which stage in oil refining is paraffin wax produced?

466 Which chemical name is abbreviated in the letters DDT?

467 Which valuable chemical is produced with phenol by the cumene route?

468 What significance have the letters ASP?

469 What is a 'sniff gas' or 'tail gas'?

470 Who discovered the polyester fibre given the trade-name 'Terylene'?

471 One of the main uses of ethylene glycol is antifreeze. What is another?

472 Which are the principal elements present in most chemical fertilisers?

473 Which class of organic chemicals may be added to give odour to natural gas?

474 Why has Tobias acid replaced 2-naphthylamine in making dyes?

475 What is 'ullage'?

476 From which naturally occurring mixture is argon derived?

477 Which has the higher boiling point, ethyl alcohol or methyl ethyl ketone?

478 What are 'bottoms' or 'heel'?

479 Which chemicals are the raw materials for the production of urea?

480 Which is the principal chemical that can be made by the Wulff Process?

DR T. F. WEST: Editor-in-Chief, Society of Chemical Industry.

481 Who said: 'Some books are to be tasted, others to be swallowed, and some few to be chewed and digested'?

482 Which race of people is considered to be the tallest in the world?

483 The Queen's Awards to Industry are announced each year – when?

484 On what type of camera would you expect to find Parallax Compensation?

485 The object of Snoopy's fantasies, who was the Red Baron?

486 Who, in legend, was the father of the Nine Muses?

487 Who was the first of the Lancastrian Kings?

488 A Phoenician goddess, she was the legendary founder of Carthage. Who was she?

489 What famous porcelain is marked with crossed swords?

490 Who, according to Greek myth, created Pandora, the first mortal woman?

491 Who was the husband of Corretta Scott?

492 What are the 'White Horses' of Westbury and Uffington?

493 What fish would you be eating if you were given Brochet au Beurre Blanc?

494 The Spanish Government moves from Madrid to which city during the summer months?

495 In the Morse Code, what combination comprises
the letter 'O'?

496 In Greek mythology, which king outwitted death?

497 Captain Cook discovered the Hawaiian Islands.
What were they originally called?

498 According to Lord Byron, 'who kill'd John Keats'?

499 'Arnolfini and his Wife' is a famous painting
by whom?

500 Which of the Gorgons in Greek mythology was
the only mortal?

Famous Russians

Set by Professor R. E. F. Smith

501 Who organised the 'Oprichnina'?

502 Who is said to have opened a window on to Europe?

503 What Russian anarchist prince spent much of his life in England?

504 Who propounded a theory of realistic acting?

505 Who said 'I know nothing more beautiful than the "Appassionata", I could hear it every day'?

506 Who was the first Soviet Commissar of Education?

507 What famous composer was a relative of Molotov?

508 Who proposed a 'new model for the universe'?

509 Name the first Romanov on the throne of Russia.

510 What polymath developed new techniques for making glass and challenged the 'Norman' theory of Russia's origins?

511 Who is the Russian author of stories about the Don Cossacks who was awarded the Nobel Prize for Literature in 1965?

512 Who almost toppled Catherine the Great from the throne?

513 Who was director (and principal playwright) of the first permanent Russian theatre?

514 What lawyer became a leader of modern abstract painting?

515 What icon painter has given his name to a recent film?

516 Who wrote *From the other shore*?

517 What Russian poet married Isadora Duncan?

518 What Russian poet married the daughter of Mendeléyev?

519 What Russian general committed suicide early in World War I?

520 Who invented 'pan-geometry'?

PROFESSOR R. E. F. SMITH: Department of Russian Language and Literature, University of Birmingham.

Geography of Great Britain

Set by Trevor Marchington

521 What are clints?

522 What is the highest peak in England and Wales?

523 Where is the Fylde?

524 What is a sarsen stone?

525 Which city is located at Latitude 53° 58′ North, Longitude 1° 5′ West?

526 What is a bourne?

527 What is Ordnance Datum?

528 Which National Park was Britain's first?

529 Name five of the crofting counties.

530 What significance had the Whin Sill for the Romans?

531 What have these places in common – Wylfa, Trawsfynyd, Hunterston?

532 What do the letters C.B.D. stand for?

533 What is the Helm wind?

534 What is the most westerly point of the mainland of Great Britain?

535 What is the Caledonian trend?

536 What is Kentish Rag?

537 What would you drive along the Parallel Roads of Glen Roy?

538 Which British landowner owns the largest acreage?

539 What does I.B.G. stand for?

540 On what map projection does the Ordnance Survey base the National Grid?

TREVOR MARCHINGTON, MA: Senior Lecturer in Geography, Shoreditch College.

General Knowledge 10

541 Mass suicide is said to have ended the defence by the zealots of which fortress?

542 What is the largest extant rodent in the world?

543 It was double-headed for Russia and Austria, single-headed for Germany. What is it?

544 To what did the Reverend Sydney Smith refer when he said, 'It is as though St Paul's had gone down to the sea, and pupped'?

545 Which English queen bore her husband fifteen children?

546 Who was the Archbishop of Canterbury at the time of King Edward VIII's abdication?

547 On what day is the October Revolution celebrated?

548 Which is the city that Lord Byron, having spent 23 days there, described as, 'my country! city of the soul!'?

549 What is the unit of currency used in Israel?

550 Eton College was founded by which monarch?

551 Alberto Santos-Dumont in 1901 won 100,000 francs for a flying achievement. What was it?

552 Its headquarters are now at Aubagne but used to be at Sidi-bel-Abbes. What is it?

553 What did the Bishop of Ely establish in 1284?

554 Where would you find the Gatun Lake, the Gaillard Cut and the Miraflores Locks?

555 Which British University was the first to admit women to degrees?

556 'How many divisions has the Pope?' is a saying that has been attributed to whom?

557 Winston Churchill and Franklin Roosevelt met on board ship in August 1941. What was the result of their meeting?

558 What did the Redcliffe-Maud Commission inquire into?

559 $MgSO_4 7H_2O$ is the chemical formula of something you can drink or bathe in. It was named after a town in England. What is this substance?

560 What is the noun of assembly for goldfinches?

English Literature

Set by Boswell Taylor

561 Who was the poet laureate who once declared:
'I must go down to the seas again, to the lonely sea
and the sky'?

562 Who was the early English scholar who composed
'The Ecclesiastical History of the English Race'?

563 What name is Dr Johnson said to have given to the
school of poets among whom are George Herbert,
Henry Vaughan and John Donne?

564 Who wrote:
'No longer mourn for me when I am dead
Than you shall hear the surly sullen bell'?

565 Who was the Professor of Latin at Cambridge who
called himself 'The Shropshire Lad'?

566 What was the work of George Chapman that inspired
one of our greatest sonnets?

567 Where did J. M. Synge find his setting for *Playboy
of the Western World*?

568 What was the title of John Bunyan's spiritual
autobiography?

569 Who is the Jesuit poet who was not 'discovered' until
nearly thirty years after his death in 1889?

570 Who dedicated a number of poems to Lucasta . . .
going beyond the Seas, going to the Wars?

571 Who was the poet who dedicated love poems to
'Jean', 'Mary' and also 'Bonnie Lesley'?

572 What is the 'scene' referred to in these famous lines
     by Marvell:
> 'He nothing common did or mean
> Upon that memorable scene'?

573 Who is the king who plays a big part in Scott's
     Quentin Durward?

574 Who is the seventeenth-century philosopher who
     wrote the classic 'An Essay Concerning Human
     Understanding'?

575 What was the 'domestic horror', to quote Walter
     Pater, that affected the life and work of
     Charles Lamb?

576 Who was the poetess sister of Dante Gabriel Rossetti?

577 Who was the mathematics tutor who wrote *Leviathan*,
     a book concerned with political theory?

578 What is the name of Prospero's island in
     The Tempest?

579 Who is the author whose formula for the novel was
     'Make 'em laugh, make 'em cry, make 'em wait'?

580 What was the Gothic novel written by Shelley's wife?

History of Music

Set by Professor Ivor Keys

581 Which Beethoven symphony was originally dedicated to Napoleon?

582 How many instruments are needed to perform Bach's Italian Concerto?

583 Who was the 'London' Bach?

584 What was the profession of Mozart's father?

585 Who was Bach's Musical Offering offered to?

586 What is the name of the sequel to the Fantastic symphony?

587 Who was Figaro's mother?

588 What composer wrote piano pieces called 'Chopin' and 'Paganini'?

589 What Weber opera has an original English libretto?

590 What orchestra was called 'an army of generals'?

591 In what other opera does Mozart quote Figaro?

592 What was Schubert's second Christian name?

593 Who wrote the music *Rule Britannia*?

594 What is the 'hateful colour' in Schubert's *Fair Maid of the Mill*?

595 Whose victory is celebrated in Beethoven's so-called Battle Symphony?

596 What is the connection between Handel and Gibraltar?

597 What work of Berlioz employs gunpowder?

598 What composer was nicknamed the Red Priest?

599 What work is inscribed thus: 'It comes from the heart: may it go to the heart'?

600 What Mozart air has piano variations by Chopin?

PROFESSOR IVOR KEYS: Department of Music, The Barber Institute of Fine Arts, Birmingham University.

General Knowledge 11

601 Which Abbey became the main meeting place for the Hell Fire Club?

602 Who wrote the brilliant pamphlet (in 1835) entitled *Vindication of the English Constitution*?

603 After what battle did Brutus commit suicide?

604 The Acropolis in Athens literally means what?

605 If you were at a meeting of SALT, what would you be discussing?

606 What are the three stanzas on which the Pindaric Ode is built?

607 What city besides Pompeii was overwhelmed in the earthquake of AD 79?

608 Whose daughter was 'The Fair Rosamund'?

609 What was the name of the flying island in *Gulliver's Travels*?

610 What is the inscription on the reverse of the Military Medal?

611 How many dimes would you get in exchange for an American dollar?

612 The name 'Irene' comes from the Greek. What does it mean?

613 What are pelagic animals?

614 What island is separated from the mainland by the Swale?

615 Why was 46 BC known as 'The year of confusion'?

616 What is the Binney Award?

617 Gainsborough painted the 'Blue Boy'. Who painted the 'Red Boy'?

618 Who collaborated with Alfred Binet in devising the first scales for measuring intelligence?

619 In the Greek alphabet A is alpha, what is E?

620 For what crimes did Oedipus blind himself?

Personalities in Russian History and the Arts

Set by Professor F. M. Borras

621 Ivan the Terrible co-operated with a group of clergy and boyars. Give its name.

622 What was the fate of the Zemsky Sobor?

623 Define the Time of Troubles.

624 Where did Peter the Great lay the foundations of the Russian capital, St Petersburg?

625 What decisive law did Peter the Great promulgate in the year 1722?

626 Who was Alexander Danilovich Menshikov?

627 What was Catherine the Great's most powerful ambition concerned with the British Empire?

628 Who was the leader of the so-called Russian parody of the Protestant reformation?

629 What were the principal aims of the Decembrist Revolution?

630 What was especially significant about the day upon which Alexander II was assassinated?

631 Who inspired the reactionary policies of Alexander III and what was his title?

632 Who suggested the name for the Revolutionary Party, the Socialist Revolutionaries?

633 Which of Pushkin's works of fiction were used as the basis for operas by Tchaikovsky?

634 What reply did Gogol's *Selected Passages from Correspondence with my Friends* evoke from a Russian critic?

635 With whom does Bazarov, Turgenev's Nihilist hero, fight a duel in *Fathers and Sons*?

636 Which Russian writer wrote a Memoir of two others whom he knew well in the Crimea?

637 In which novel does Dostoevsky describe the pretence that he was to be executed?

638 Who resigned from the Academy of Sciences upon the Tsar's rejection of Gorky's election to it?

639 Who was awarded the Nobel Prize for Literature while in exile?

640 Which Russian writer's obituary appeared twice in *The Times*?

PROFESSOR F. M. BORRAS: Head of the Department of Russian Studies, Leeds University.

English Cathedrals

Set by Professor J. G. Davies

641 Who was responsible for the foundation of Salisbury cathedral?

642 What was Paul's Walk?

643 In which cathedral is there a tablet commemorating Nurse Cavell?

644 On the west façade of one cathedral there are statues of eleven kings from William the Conqueror to Edward III. Which cathedral is it?

645 In which cathedral is there a font of Tournai marble depicting three scenes from the life of St Nicholas of Myra?

646 Who was the architect of the Anglican cathedral in Liverpool?

647 In which cathedral is the tomb of King John (d. 1216)?

648 On the tomb on King John there is a carving of a lion biting the end of a sword. To what is this said to refer?

649 Legend has it that after the murder of St Ethelbert by Offa of Mercia (*c.* 794), his ghost demanded burial in a certain place which is now the site of a cathedral. Which cathedral is it?

650 Which English cathedral is also a college chapel?

651 For what order of monks was Rochester cathedral originally built?

652 In St Alban's cathedral there is a watching loft. What was it used for?

653 Which cathedral of medieval origin has neither triforium nor clerestory?

654 Which cathedral is dedicated to St Saviour?

655 In which part of Canterbury cathedral was Thomas à Becket murdered?

656 High up on the wall of the nave is carved a grotesque face to scare away demons from spying on the monks. In which cathedral is it to be found?

657 In which cathedral is there a chantry chapel decorated with owls?

658 What is the position of the bishop's chair in Norwich cathedral?

659 Who designed the stained-glass window by the font in the new Coventry cathedral?

660 Where is the earliest example of fan-vaulting?

PROFESSOR J. G. DAVIES, MA, DD: Institute for the Study of Worship and Religious Architecture, University of Birmingham.

General Knowledge 12

661   Tallinn is its largest city and capital. What is the name of this state?

662   Who succeeded Vic Feather as General Secretary of the Trades Union Council?

663   He was a Scholastic Theologian born in 1225, known as Doctor Angelicus. Who was he?

664   Which family holds the hereditary right to the Office of Earl Marshal of England?

665   Which Italian premier signed the armistice with the Allies in 1943?

666   From which century are the Paston Letters?

667   Sir Winston Churchill was a war correspondent during the South African war. For which paper did he write?

668   Where was King Arthur taken after he was mortally wounded?

669   Lord Frederick Cavendish and Thomas Henry Burke were assassinated. What has this tragedy become known as?

670   Who was the sculptor responsible for the lions at the base of Nelson's Column in Trafalgar Square?

671   Des Moines is the capital of which American State?

672   What sea does the Volga empty into?

673   Thomas Moore's poem 'Meeting of the Waters' immortalised which village?

674 Who was the Greek philosopher who believed that only atoms and empty space exist?

675 Which is the largest of the Trucial States?

676 What was the name of Shylock's wife?

677 He was British Commandant of the Arab Legion's Desert Patrol between 1939 and 1956. Who is he?

678 In which of Shakespeare's plays would you find Costard, a clown?

679 Who created the gardens at Versailles?

680 Bernard Shaw wrote the part of Eliza Doolittle especially for which actress?

British Church Architecture

Set by Bruce Allsopp

681 Of what period is a lancet window typical?

682 What is Boston Stump?

683 What is a porticus?

684 Who was the architect of St Martin-in-the-Fields, Trafalgar Square, London?

685 Where are the earliest existing ribbed high vaults in England?

686 What Anglo-Saxon church tower has a helm roof?

687 Which cathedral has a free-standing tower on the north side?

688 What is the literal meaning of 'basilica'?

689 Who was the designer of the nave of Canterbury Cathedral?

690 What is the chapter house of Southwell Minster specially famous for?

691 Which cathedral has an octagonal timber lantern over the crossing?

692 Who designed the stained-glass windows behind the high altar of St Paul's Cathedral, London?

693 Who was the architect of Westminster Cathedral?

694 What church imitated in its structural form an up-turned Viking ship?

695 What is a mason's mitre?

696 St Wilfred was said to have built the largest church north of the Alps. Where?

697 What are 'commissioners' churches'?

698 What connection is there between St Mary's Cathedral, Newcastle-upon-Tyne, and a hansom cab?

699 Who was the architect of St Giles-in-the-Fields, Holborn, London?

700 What is an arch-lintel?

BRUCE ALLSOPP: Reader in the History of Architecture, University of Newcastle-upon-Tyne.

Grand Opera

Set by Harold Rosenthal

701   How did Covent Garden Opera House get its name?

702   What was the Shakespearian opera Verdi wanted to write all his life, but never actually got round to doing?

703   Who completed Puccini's *Turandot* after the composer had died?

704   What was the 'Grand Boutique'?

705   On whom did Wagner base the character of Beckmesser in *The Mastersingers*?

706   What is verismo?

707   When the *Ring* had its first performance at Covent Garden in 1892, conducted by Mahler, it was not given in the correct order. Why was this?

708   In what opera do we meet the stage manager of the Comédie Française?

709   The characters Manrico, Florestan and Don Alvaro share three things in common - what are they?

710   Name a famous singer who collapsed and died on stage during a performance.

711   What is the difference between opéra comique (without a hyphen) and opéra-comique with a hyphen?

712   During the première of which famous opera did a cat walk across the stage?

713   Who wrote the libretto for Verdi's *Otello*?

714 Which opera is based on Ben Jonson's *Epicoene*?

715 Which was the first opera of Verdi?

716 What do the Puccini Mimi, Tosca and Butterfly all have in common – besides, of course, being sopranos and the heroines of their respective operas?

717 The title of one of Verdi's familiar operas is mentioned by one of the characters in a very well-known opera by Mozart. What are the two operas?

718 Who are known as La Stupenda and La Superba?

719 In Tchaikovsky's *The Queen of Spades* the old Countess sings a little song by another composer – who?

720 Who taught Walther von Stolzing how to sing?

HAROLD ROSENTHAL: Editor of *Opera*.

721 What was Operation Dynamo in the Second World War?

722 Name one of the Angevin Kings of England.

723 In which calendar would the year 1974 be numbered 1394?

724 Which country was the first to open a scheduled passenger air service?

725 Which one-act ballet is set in a toy-shop?

726 This British Prime Minister entered the House of Commons as MP for Limehouse in 1922. Who was he?

727 What Bishop (in 1654) placed the date of the Creation in 4004 BC?

728 When offered his freedom his answer was always the same: 'If you set me free today, I will preach again tomorrow'. Who was he?

729 Which Greek philosopher is said to be the founder of the atomic theory?

730 Ships are warned of rocks to the west of Alderney in the Channel Islands by a lighthouse. Which one?

731 In 1866 William Steinitz became a world champion. Of what?

732 From what kind of animal is rennet obtained?

733 Who was the American actor who turned film director and was responsible for the two three-hour silent epics – *The Birth of a Nation* and *Intolerance*?

734 Name the smallest of Switzerland's Cantons.

735 What was the title of the opera Berlioz based on Shakespeare's *Much Ado About Nothing*?

736 The old halfpenny coin had a ship on the reverse side. Which famous ship inspired this design?

737 What do the initials B.M.E.W.S. stand for?

738 In what year in the 19th century did Europe see widespread revolutions?

739 On which island is Fingal's Cave?

740 By what is the Great Ape Pongo Pygmaeus commonly known?

History of World Theatre

Set by Simon Trussler

741 Who is the odd-man-out among these four famous Greek dramatists: Aeschylus, Aristophanes, Euripides, Sophocles?

742 Name the *two* dramatists who have written the best-known plays concerning the Faust Legend.

743 Who wrote *An Enemy of the People*?

744 Name the two Elizabethan actors who were responsible for the collection of Shakespeare's plays into the First Folio of 1723.

745 Name the dramatist whose political satires prompted the passing of the Licensing Act of 1737, which imposed the Lord Chamberlain's censorship over stage plays.

746 Name the play by J. M. Synge which provoked a riot at its first performance at Dublin's Abbey Theatre in 1907.

747 Whose theoretical writings *originated* the recently-revived concept of a 'theatre of cruelty'.

748 Who wrote the music for Bertolt Brecht's *The Threepenny Opera*?

749 To which equally famous actor is the French actress Madeleine Renaud married?

750 Which play 'made Gay rich and Rich gay'?

751 Who wrote *Waiting for Lefty*?

752 Which recently-opened London theatre is named after a famous Irish playwright?

753 Which member of a famous theatrical family made his first appearance in 1921 as the Herald in *Henry V*, and was knighted in 1953?

754 What is the name of the American experimental theatre group directed since its formation in 1947 by Julian Beck and Judith Malina?

755 Name two of the four English towns whose cycles of medieval mystery plays have survived more or less intact.

756 Which were the two London theatres whose 'letters patent' theoretically entitled them to a monopoly of 'straight plays' until 1843?

757 Which pop singer appeared at the Old Vic in 1960 as Tony Lumpkin in Goldsmith's *She Stoops to Conquer*?

758 Who was the first Artistic Director of the English Stage Company at the Royal Court Theatre after its formation in 1956?

759 What are the *christian names* of the Italian actor and playwright brothers, De Filippo?

760 The memoirs of probably the best-known of English pantomime clowns were edited by Charles Dickens. Who was he?

SIMON TRUSSLER: editor, *Oxford Companion of the Theatre*.

19th-Century English History

Set by John D. Bareham

761 Which Act made the Secret Ballot effective and prevented electoral corruption?

762 Which Prime Minister died in office at the age of almost 81?

763 Which British subject, born a Portuguese Jew, made claims against the Greek Government in 1849–50?

764 Approximately how much money did the Whig Education Grant of 1833 make available to Church School Societies?

765 Who was Gladstone's Secretary for War who carried through a series of Army Reforms?

766 What were the three 'Fs' of the Irish?

767 At what rate did Peel levy his reintroduced income tax?

768 What clause in 1870 gave parents the right to withdraw children from prayers and scripture lessons in schools?

769 Explain the initials G.O.M. and M.O.G. used for Gladstone.

770 Which Minister was largely responsible for the detail of the many basic social reform acts of 1875–6?

771 What were the contents of the 'Extraordinary Black Book' of 1831?

772 Which writer spread the idea from 1859 that by thrift and hard work any moral person could rise to eminence?

773 Who remained Commander-in-Chief of the British Army for 40 years?

774 Which corporation remained unreformed throughout the 19th century?

775 Whom did Disraeli describe as 'an old, painted pantaloon, very deaf, very blind . . . '?

776 What was the main function of local party organisations down to 1914?

777 What important census was held in 1851 in addition to the normal ten-yearly one?

778 Which English novelist held official positions in South Africa in 1875–9, and hoisted the Union Jack over Pretoria in 1879?

779 Which historian claimed that the English had colonised half the world 'in a fit of absence of mind'?

780 Which Company sent the Government a bill for over £500 after the 1848 Chartist disturbances?

JOHN D. BAREHAM, BA: Head of History and Economic History Sections, Exeter College.

The Iliad and the Odyssey

Set by Dr Wolfgang Liebeschuetz

781 Who was the first man to shelter the returned Odysseus in Ithaca?

782 Why is the Iliad so named?

783 Who was the Gerenian horseman?

784 Who was forced to kiss the hands that had slain his sons?

785 By what sign did Eurycleia recognise Odysseus?

786 What topic is announced at the beginning of the Iliad?

787 What was the effect of the Cyclops Polyphemus' cursing of Odysseus?

788 What way of life did Achilles consider the most miserable on earth?

789 What was the shape adopted by Athene and Apollo to watch Hector challenging the Greeks?

790 Which hero compared the generations of men to the leaves of trees?

791 The son of a hero was frightened by his father wearing a helmet. Name the boy.

792 The Trojan war might have been stopped as a result of a duel between Menelaus and Paris. Which Trojan prevented this?

793 Two extremely happy men wailed like vultures whose young have been taken from the nest. Who were they?

794 Which god was most hateful to Zeus?

795 What was the name of the horse which foretold Achilles' death?

796 What was a hippocampus?

797 Name the American scholar who proved that the *Iliad* and *Odyssey* are oral compositions.

798 Ajax's shield 'like a tower' could shelter an archer behind it. When were such shields used in Greece?

799 A line of battle is described as 'a hedge of spears and shields, buckler to buckler, helmet to helmet ...' (*Iliad, XIII*, 130–5). When were these tactics introduced in Greece?

800 Who is the divine messenger in the *Iliad*?

DR WOLFGANG LIEBESCHUETZ: Department of Classics, Leicester University.

General Knowledge 14

801 What was the non-military role of Admiral Horthy?

802 Darwin was a scientist on board the *Beagle*. Who was the famous biologist who served as a medical officer on *HMS Rattlesnake*?

803 According to legend where were the Kings of Ireland crowned?

804 Electrical resistance is measured by the ohm. What unit measures the reciprocal of resistance, which is conductance?

805 Born in Paris in 1908, she won the Prix Goncourt with her novel *The Mandarins*. Who is she?

806 Voltaire's character Candide witnessed the execution of an Admiral. Upon which real event was this based?

807 In the play *Who's Afraid of Virginia Woolf* George was the husband. Who was the wife?

808 Who were 'the great Twin Brothers to whom all Dorians pray'?

809 Who was responsible for the building of the Pantheon in Rome?

810 Of what nationality was Malthus, the theorist on population?

811 What is marzipan made of?

812 Where is the GPO communications satellite/earth station which relayed the first television pictures by satellite?

813 Who was the poet who perfected 'Sprung' and 'Counterpoint' rhythms?

814 A famous allegory was written in Bedford gaol. What was the title?

815 Why was the awarding of the Scottish Cup withheld in 1908–9?

816 A useless piece of labour is sometimes called a 'Sisyphean task'. Why?

817 Her name is the title of an opera by Richard Strauss, a Jean Giraudoux play and a Michael Cacoyannis film. Who is she?

818 Which country administers the territory known as the Ross Dependency?

819 Who is the author of *King Solomon's Ring*?

820 Who was Freud's notable disciple who developed the concept of the birth trauma?

Classical Mythology

Set by Dr Wolfgang Liebeschuetz

821 Which day of the week includes the name of a Roman god?

822 Which god was described as the 'earth shaker'?

823 What was the name of the Cyclops blinded by Odysseus?

824 Where was Dido born?

825 What is a Dryad?

826 What mythological people lived on the island of Corfu?

827 Who was the hero who went mad outside Troy, slaughtering first a herd of sheep then himself?

828 Who was the muse of epic poetry?

829 He founded Thebes and was turned into a serpent. Give his name.

830 What was the origin of the Titans?

831 What is the title of a poem of Hesiod which describes the origin of the gods?

832 Apollo threw a discus and killed the boy he loved. Who was the boy?

833 An uncle fed his nephews' flesh to their father. Who was the father?

834 One of the seven heroes fleeing from Thebes was swallowed by the earth. What was his name?

835   Justice once lived among men. Later she fled and became a constellation. What is the name of this constellation?

836   Who was required to bring back from Hades a casket full of the beauty of Persephone?

837   A weaver wove the love-life of the gods. Who was this weaver who was turned into a spider?

838   What god had an oracle at Dodona?

839   Why was the mother of Dionysus reduced to ashes?

840   During a sacrifice girls wore saffron robes and pretended to be bears. Who was the goddess who was worshipped at this ceremony?

DR WOLFGANG LIEBESCHUETZ: Department of Classics, Leicester University.

Arthurian Literature

Set by T. A. Shippey

841 Which knight, in English sources, throws away
Excalibur?

842 Which three knights of Arthur achieved the Holy
Grail?

843 What name does Malory give to Arthur's mother?

844 At which battle did Arthur kill 960 of the enemy
single-handed?

845 Who was Lucius Hiberius?

846 In which century did Geoffrey of Monmouth write
the *History of the Kings of Britain*?

847 In which century did Saint Gildas write of the
battle of Mount Badon?

848 Which knight struck the dolorous stroke that laid
waste three Kingdoms?

849 What was the real name of the Green Knight who
played at beheading with Sir Gawain?

850 What did Sir Erec or Sir Geraint forbid his wife to do?

851 Why did Sir Gawain swear revenge on Sir Lancelot
to the death?

852 What animal caused by accident the last battle
between Arthur and Mordred?

853 What was the relationship between Arthur and
Mordred?

854 Which knight did Sir Lancelot fight without helmet or
shield, and with his left hand behind his back?

855 If Arthur's sword was Calibeorn, and his shield Pridwen, what was the name of his spear?

856 In which poem are we told of a warrior: 'he glutted black ravens on the rampart of the fort, though he was not Arthur'?

857 Whose task was it to pursue the Questing Beast, or Beast Glatisant?

858 In a modern work King Arthur has to undergo an ordeal in the shape of a hawk. What is the ordeal?

859 In a tournament at Winchester Sir Lancelot wore a red sleeve embroidered with pearls. Whose was it?

860 In Tennyson's *Gareth and Lynette*, what is the secret of the Black Knight, Death?

T. A. SHIPPEY, MA: St John's College, Oxford.

General Knowledge 15

861 What is the famous work that followed the researches of a scientist on the Galapagos Islands?

862 His name was Joel Chandler Harris. What was the nom-de-plume he adopted when he told his stories about Brer Rabbit and Brer Fox?

863 Who was the reluctant American vice-presidential candidate who was described as 'the contrariest Missouri mule I've ever dealt with'?

864 What is the chemical element found in all proteins?

865 Who was the Swiss psychiatrist who gave his name to a personality test which directs the subject's attention to ink blots?

866 What is the bird that aroused Wordsworth to question whether it could be called a bird 'or but a wandering voice'?

867 There are some strange subjects for dictionaries. What was the subject of a dictionary compiled by Ambrose Bierce?

868 In British folk-lore, who was the monster slain by Beowulf?

869 An element has an atomic number of 26 and it has 30 neutrons. What is its atomic weight?

870 Two men shared the power in Russia for a time after Khrushchev fell. Who were they?

871 What is the name that housewives give to the substance that chemists call sodium hydroxide?

872 Who changed the misogynist Sultan Shahriyar and turned him into a happily married man, and by what means?

873 What is the acronym for light amplification by stimulated emission of radiation?

874 A symbol of atomic power stands on the place at the University of Chicago where man experimented with the control of atomic energy. Who sculpted this monument?

875 'Defenestration' was the old Bohemian custom that sparked off the Thirty Years War. What happened to the victim?

876 What are getting old when they are worn down to monadnocks and peneplanes?

877 What is the republic that was first a settlement following the landing of Jan van Riebeeck at Table Bay in 1652?

878 Who described Russia as 'a riddle, wrapped in a mystery, inside an enigma'?

879 Who is recorded as having said that 'no man but a blockhead ever wrote except for money'?

880 What is the disease that was sometimes known as St Anthony's fire?

Kings and Queens of England

Set by John D. Bareham

881 Which exiled English king was lent the Palace of St Germain-en-Laye by Louis XIV?

882 Which king suppressed Oldcastle and the Lollards?

883 What nickname is given to Queen Elizabeth I's last speech to a deputation from the House of Commons?

884 Name the two husbands of the Empress Matilda.

885 Which English king was buried under a cathedral tower which collapsed the next year?

886 What was the other nickname of Richard Coeur de Lion?

887 Where were Henry II and his queen buried?

888 What did Charles II offer the English Parliament in 1649 in a vain attempt to save his father's life?

889 Which English king was said by his son to have 'a gruff blue-water approach to all human problems'?

890 What 'wrestler' defeated Henry VIII in France in 1520?

891 Who was the mother of Charles II's illegitimate son, the Duke of Monmouth?

892 What is now considered most likely to have caused George III's so-called madness?

893 On what subject did Edward VII as Prince of Wales make his only full speech in the House of Lords?

894 What was Jane Grey's 'claim' to the English throne in 1553?

895 Who was Elizabeth I's 'little black husband'?

896 On what first occasion after the death of Prince Albert did Victoria again dance the Valse?

897 Which English monarch attended more Cabinet meetings than any other?

898 What did William IV offer when the Houses of Parliament were destroyed by fire in 1833?

899 What is the meaning of 'porphyrogeniture'?

900 Which Plantagenet, according to Maurice Ashley, established the 'nucleus of a royal navy' by having galleys specially built?

JOHN D. BAREHAM, BA: Head of History and Economic History Sections, Exeter College.

Shakespeare's Plays

Set by Boswell Taylor

901 Who was the Shakespearian heroine who disguised herself as Ganymede, after 'Jove's own page'?

902 Who described the Earl of Gloucester as 'the foul fiend Flibbertigibbet'?

903 Which play has 'Cupid and Amazons in the Masque' among its dramatis personae?

904 Whose servants are Nathaniel, Joseph, Nicholas, Philip, Walter and Sugarsop?

905 Of whom is Hamlet thinking when he says: 'Frailty, thy name is woman'?

906 Which play begins: 'In delivering my son from me, I bury a second husband'?

907 Who, at his life's end, played with flowers and smiled upon his fingers' ends?

908 In *Cymbeline*, what future is prophesied for Britain by the Soothsayer?

909 In *The Merchant of Venice*, of what was the casket made that bore the words: *Who chooseth me must give and hazard all he hath*?

910 Who was the father of Katharina and Bianca?

911 In which city is 'the moated Grange at St Luke's' a scene setting?

912 Who, when asked by royalty what he would eat, requested a peck of provender . . . good dry oats . . . and good hay, sweet hay?

913 In which play do we get the song 'Who is Sylvia?'

914 Who was 'a fellow of infinite jest, of most excellent fancy'?

915 Who declared that he was as 'pretty a piece of flesh as any in Messina' but wished that he 'had been writ down an ass!'?

916 What was the basket said to contain besides the asp that killed Cleopatra?

917 Who dies saying 'the rest is silence'?

918 Who was 'the fantastical Spaniard'?

919 What did Prince Hal call a 'polish'd perturbation! golden care!'?

920 What is Elbow in *Measure for Measure*?

Answers

General Knowledge 1

1 On the fourth day.

2 Antonine Wall.

3 Iceland. (The older of the two is the Elder (or Poetic) Edda written about 1270 and the other is Sronri Sturhuson's Younger (or Prose) Edda.)

4 Chief Sitting Bull of the Sioux, or Crazy Horse (they were joint leaders, but Sitting Bull was the medicine man and Crazy Horse the field leader. In 1876, better known as Custer's Last Stand).

5 Adonis.

6 Montevideo, Uruguay, 1930.

7 Mali, at the southern boundary of the Sahara.

8 Varieties of bricks.

9 American War of Independence (surrendered to the Americans at Yorktown in 1781).

10 Members of the Sioux Indian Tribe (Siege of Wounded Knee).

11 James Monroe (1758–1831).

12 Bleeding Heart.

13 John Prebble.

14 King Henry I (by the measurement from his nose to his thumb).

15 Jasper Petulengro.

16 Launching missiles (rocks). It was a siege engine.

17 Followers of (The Schoolman) Dune Scotus (c. 1265/1308). (The word 'Dunce' is derived from his birthplace, Dunse.)

18 Eight. (The programme has run for over 30 years and must be known to every listener in the land.)

19   The Furies (Erinyes or Eumenides).

20   George Bernard Shaw (*The Rejected Statement*, Part One).

Astronomy

21   Jupiter.

22   It always points more or less away from the Sun – so that when a comet is receding from the Sun it travels tail-first.

23   An eclipsing variable – sometimes, more properly, called an eclipsing binary. (Its apparent fluctuations of light are due to the fact that it is made up of two stars, revolving round their common centre of gravity; when the fainter star passes in front of the brighter, as happens every $2\frac{1}{2}$ days, Algol seems to give a long, slow 'wink'.)

24   The *Mare Tranquillitatis*, or Sea of Tranquillity.

25   James Gregory. (*Not* Newton, who did however build the first reflector some years later. Gregory's pattern was rather different from Newton's, and Gregory never actually attempted the construction.)

26   Mercury and Venus (which are closer to the Sun than we are).

27   A quasar, which is beyond our Galaxy, whereas a pulsar is contained in our own Galaxy.

28   Mariner 10, in 1974.

29   Vesta. (Not the largest, which is Ceres. Only Vesta among the asteroids is ever visible with the naked eye.)

30   Halley's Comet.

31   It is either new or full.

32   The Perseids.

33   An F-type star is *yellowish*; a K-star, orange.

34 Titan, the largest satellite of Saturn. (The ground atmospheric pressure is probably about 100 mb., or ten times greater than that on the surface of Mars.)

35 The *Mare Serenitatis* (Sea of Serenity).

36 On Mars.

37 The Great Spiral in Andromeda – an external galaxy at a distance of 2.2 million light-years from us.

38 Ole Romer.

39 Neptune.

40 On Mercury. (This is a bright ray-crater, identified from the Mariner 10 pictures in March 1974. Dr Kuiper died in 1974.)

Legends of Britain

41 Brut or Brute or Brutus.

42 Troy. (Said to be the grandson of Aeneas of Troy.)

43 Merlin's.
'She is not any common earth
Water or wood or air,
But Merlin's Isle of Gramarye
Where you and I will fare.'
(Gramarye meaning occult, magic (OED). From Sir Walter Scott, revived by him in 1740.)

44 Vortigern or Guorthigirnus or Wyrtgeorn (the first is the common pronunciation and spelling). (More legend than historical fact, but certainly well established as a legend. Vortigern was a Celtic king. Possibly invited Germans under Hengest to assist him against attacks. Said to have married Rowena, daughter of Hengest.)

45 He crossed running water.
'So Maggie (the mare) runs, the witches follow . . .
A runnin' stream they dare na cross . . . '

46 Guy of Warwick. (In *Guy of Warwick*, an English verse romance of the 14th century, Guy rescued King Athelstan from the Danes under Anlaf, defeating the Danish champion near Winchester.)

47 Peterborough.

48 A creature part seal, part man.

49 St Dunstan.

50 Havelock the Dane. (Hero of stories which appeared about 1290. After the death of his father, King Birkabeyn, the Earl of Godard ordered that Havelock should be drowned. A fisherman named Grim fled with the boy to England.)

51 Huntingdon.

52 Friar Bacon (and Friar Bungay). (In Robert Green's *Friar Bacon and Friar Bungay*. The friars are magicians. The 'brazen head' is destroyed by a mysterious power as soon as it attained to speech.)

53 A water-demon, usually in the shape of a horse.

54 Female cannibalistic hags and/or river spirits.

55 Pwyll. (The *Four Branches of Mabinogi* is a recognised source of Welsh legends. The first of the Four Branches tells the story of Pwyll.)

56 The Picts or Pechs.

57 Perthshire (at Fortingall). (Quoted in county histories, AA information sheets, etc. Fortingall yew cited in *Guinness Book of Records* as oldest tree in Britain.)

58 The Lambton Worm. (From a well-known north-east ballad. Lambton catches the Worm, the Worm escapes from the well, and in a final combat between the two, the Worm loses out.)

59 At Christmas.

60 Joseph of Arimathea. (Referred to by Malory and T. H. White. First introduced into medieval romances about 1200 by Robert de Borron.)

General Knowledge 2

61 Selene, the Greek moon-goddess who fell in love with the sleeping Endymion.

62 A compound of mercury (mercurous nitrate), which was used in the manufacture of felt hats; its effects could produce St Vitus's Dance and other symptoms. (Lewis Carroll only popularised the phrase; it is found earlier in Thackeray's *Pendennis* (in 1848) and earlier still in American literature.)

63 E. M. Forster (collaborated with Eric Crozier).

64 The Cor Anglais.

65 St James's Palace. (It became the official residence of the sovereign from 1698, when Whitehall Palace was destroyed by fire, until 1837 when Queen Victoria made Buckingham Palace the official residence.)

66 Shang (or Yin), *c.* 1766–*c.* 1123 BC. (Two royal houses earlier than the Shang have been mentioned – Yu and Hsia – but their historicity has not been determined.)

67 Nelson. (Then a Vice-Admiral, under the command of Sir Hyde Parker.)

68 Henry VII and Henry VIII. (This is also true of American packs.)

69 Jean Honoré Fragonard.

70 The Organisation of Latin American Solidarity (*Organizacion Latinoamericana de Solidaridad*). (Inspired by Castro, the movement aims to model the whole of South America on the Cuban pattern by revolution.)

71 William Makepeace Thackeray.

72 Winkles (periwinkles).

73 Tricoteuses. (Also, but less commonly, known as the Furies of the Guillotine.)

74   Alex Olmedo in 1959.

75   Forget-me-not (blue, pink or white flowers).

76   Six.

77   *Brief Encounter*.

78   Puddle Dock.

79   Sergei Eisenstein (made in the USSR in 1925).

80   French Guinea, which therefore became independent.

20th-Century British Politics

81   Andrew Bonar Law (23 October 1922 to 20 May 1923).

82   Mark Bonham Carter's win at Torrington
      (27 March 1958).

83   17 years. (From the formation of the Campbell
      Bannerman Liberal Government in December 1905
      to the fall of his own government on 19 October 1922).

84   In May 1929, under the terms of the Representation
      of the People Act of 1928.

85   Jim Griffiths (appointed by the new Labour
      Government in October 1964).

86   Dr Robert McIntyre (elected in a by-election on
      12 April 1945 and defeated in the general election
      three months later).

87   Under a 1949 Act the industry was first nationalised
      on 1 January 1951. It was denationalised in 1953 and
      renationalised on 28 July 1967.

88   Philip Snowden, Chancellor of the Exchequer in the
      newly formed National Government (on
      21 September 1931).

89   1945. (When all obervers were assuming a Churchill
      victory, the Gallup poll in the *News Chronicle* got
      the Labour landslide in votes almost exactly right.)

90   Five. (Oldham 1899, Manchester 1908, Dundee 1922, Leicester 1923, Westminster (Abbey Division) 1924.)

91   David Lloyd George (in December 1916).

92   Sir Stafford Cripps on 4 February 1948.

93   It was the scene of a naval 'mutiny' in September 1931 in protest against pay reductions.

94   Permanent head of the treasury.

95   David Lloyd George (May 1915 to July 1916).

96   Harold Macmillan in 1958.

97   They were all represented by Conservative Prime Ministers (Baldwin, Eden, Heath).

98   1912 (£400 a year).

99   A judgement in 1901 that Trade Unions could be sued for damages caused by strikes. It was revenged by the Trades Disputes Act of 1906 but it gave impetus to the launching of the Labour party.

100 In 1910–11 the ditchers were those Conservative Peers who were prepared to die in the last ditch in the fight against cuts in the House of Lords powers. Those who were willing to compromise became known as the hedgers.

Science Fiction

101 The worst thing in the world: in this case, rats (George Orwell, *1984*).

102 Mercenary soldiers (Dickson, *Dorsai!*, etc.).

103 Brazil (John Wyndham & Lucas Parkes, *The Outward Urge*).

104 R – for Robot (Isaac Asimov, *The Caves of Steel*).

105 Luck: she was born lucky (Larry Niven, *Ringworld*).

106 Brian Aldiss's *Hothouse*.

108   *Answers to questions 90–124*

107 Jack Vance's *The Dragon Masters*.

108 Bob Shaw (*Other Days, Other Eyes*).

109 Harry Harrison's *A Transatlantic Tunnel, Hurrah!*

110 Philip K. Dick's *The Man in the High Castle*.

111 He was 'the man who sold the moon' (Robert Heinlein, *The Man who Sold the Moon*).

112 Kimball Kinnison (Smith, *Gray Lensman*, etc.).

113 He was caught 'booklegging', i.e. smuggling books (Walter Miller, *A Canticle for Leibowitz*).

114 A. E. van Vogt's *Dormant*.

115 Murray Leinster (*S.O.S. from Three Worlds*, etc.).

116 Old North Australia, or Norstrilia (Cordwainer Smith, *Mother Hitton's Littul Kittons*).

117 A. C. Clarke's *Childhood's End*.

118 Kurt Vonnegut's *Cat's Cradle*.

119 The Aerial Board of Control.

120 Being used to living under 700 gravities, he assumed that all falls were fatal (Hal Clement, *Mission of Gravity*).

General Knowledge 3

121 The boundary between the Earth's crustal and mantle rocks. (The Earth's interior is divided into 3 chief layers: a liquid core, a surrounding mantle and a thin crust. The upper boundary of the mantle is thought to be the Mohorovičić Discontinuity, sometimes called the Moho, or M. Discovered in 1909 by Yugoslav seismologist A. Mohorovičić.)

122 Bernadette's vision of Our Lady.

123 Ralph Johnson Bunche in 1950.

124 *Graf Spee* (also called the *Admiral Graf Spee*. Scuttled off Montevideo on 17 December).

125 Ali Baba and the Forty Thieves. (First performed 1916.)

126 In a theatre (the side from which an artist receives a prompt – generally but not always on the right-hand side facing the audience).

127 Henry Green.

128 Four years.

129 German. (Georg Simon Ohm, who gave his name to the unit of electrical resistance.)

130 Sir John Lubbock (later Baron Avebury). He promoted the Bank Holidays Act, 1871.

131 Mandarin (Potonghua).

132 Hissarlik.

133 Singapore, by Lt-Gen. Percival.

134 Edinburgh Castle (made at Mons in Flanders).

135 Tycho Brahe.

136 Toltecs. (The Toltec civilisation was very much in decline at the beginning of the 12th century AD whilst the Aztecs were searching for a place to settle.)

137 Julian, a Roman Emperor, renounced his Christianity and adopted pagan beliefs.

138 A cable (or cable length). (The nautical mile is 6080 feet.)

139 Ra (sometimes Re or Phra). (Curiously there is another Sun God Ra, in Raiatea in Polynesia.)

140 Carapace. (Carapace is sometimes extended to the hard case investing the body in some other animals, e.g. certain Infusoria, a class of Protozoa.)

Gilbert and Sullivan

141 Angelina.

142 From: eggs, ham, mustard and cress, strawberry jam, (rollicking) bun, muffin, toast, Sally Lunn.

143 Sir Roderic Murgatroyd, who marries Dame Hannah.

144 (a) Legal, (b) aesthetic, (c) feminist.

145 Climbing over rocky mountains.

146 Belgrave Square and Seven Dials. (Sung by the Peers pleading their suit to Phyllis in *Iolanthe*.)

147 She married Colonel Fairfax, and was paid 100 crowns.

148 Sir Clarence Poltwhistle.

149 Marco marries Gianetta and Giuseppe marries Tessa.

150 The Royal English Opera House, later known as the Palace Theatre; the opera was *Ivanhoe*.

151 *Thespis*.

152 Left shoulder blade.

153 He falsified an income tax return, forged a will, shot a fox, forged a cheque and disinherited his unborn son.

154 It was a bank holiday.

155 Arac, Guron, Scynthius.

156 His sisters and his cousins and his aunts.

157 Stick close to your desks and never go to sea And you all may be Rulers of the Queen's Navy.

158 The Royal Bijou Theatre, Paignton.

159 The Opera Comique, 3 April 1880.

160 Captain Shaw of the London Fire Brigade.

Greek Mythology

161 Owl.

162 He was shot by Paris with Apollo guiding the arrow.

163 Argos.

164 Hephaestus.

165 She would prophesy truth but no one would believe it.

166 Aegisthus.

167 Pentheus.

168 Pan.

169 Danae.

170 The Centaurs had tried to rape the Lapiths' women.

171 Alcmena.

172 19 out of 50.

173 Philomela. (This is the usual version, but in one ancient author Philomela's sister Procne is transformed into a nightingale.)

174 So that his father, Cronos, should not hear his cries.

175 Bellerophon.

176 Ares.

177 Passiphae and a bull.

178 Water from a spring on Mount Helicon.

179 The island of Thera.

180 Eleusis.

General Knowledge 4

181 Whigs who rebelled against the Liberal Government's proposals for further Parliamentary reform in 1866.

182 A dog that pursues its quarry into the *earth* or *unearths* its prey. (From the Latin 'terra' = earth, via medieval Latin 'terrarius'.)

183 A celestial bull was sent to destroy him. (He was Gilgamesh.)

184 Edward H. Bailey.

185 Temple of Diana. (Excavations at Ephesus, between 1863 and 1874.)

186 In Izaak Walton's *The Compleat Angler*.

187 Iceland. (Ruled by Denmark until then.)

188 Sayonara. (Not to be confused with cyanide, which is good-bye in any language!)

189 Tolstoy's *War and Peace*.

190 1848.

191 'The Fates.' (Their names were Lachesis, Clotho, Atropos. Moirae was the Greek original, Parcae the Latin equivalent.)

192 Clydesdale, Shire, Suffolk, Percheron.

193 Botswana Republic.

194 Lewis Carroll's manuscript of *Alice's Adventures Underground*. (Later published with added material to make it twice the length as *Alice's Adventures in Wonderland*.)

195 Quinces. (Word derives from Portuguese 'marmelo' = quince.)

196 Cotton. (A Gin is a machine for separating cotton from its seeds.)

197 *Lord of the Rings* by J. R. R. Tolkien.

198   A stole (a narrow strip of silk or linen).

199   The rim of the wheel (the curved piece of wood which, joined with others, forms the rim).

200   George Hepplewhite.

British Ornithology

201   Wishbone or Merrythought.

202   Also called *ala spuria* or bastard wing. It is a tuft of small quill feathers attached to the first digit of the wing; used in flight, especially by birds of prey, to prevent stalling, and by some ducks when swimming.

203   A plumage resembling that of the female adopted for a short period in late summer by many male ducks (drakes) and often accompanied by temporary loss of flight feathers.

204   The mute swan *Cygnus olor* has about 20,000.

205   The projection on the lower mandible of certain birds, especially in Britain the large gulls, in which it is coloured red, in contrast to the yellow bill. Its purpose is to attract the chick to take food from the parent's bill.

206   The young of a nidifugous bird leave the nest within a few hours or less of hatching; examples are ducks, waders, game birds. Also called 'precocial' in America.

207   The female lacks the small red patch at nape of neck.

208   The fruit or 'keys' of the ash *Fraxinus excelsior*.

209   Because he is considered to be a third less in size than the female, often called the 'falcon'. From Latin tertius = third.

210   Scientific name of genus of nightjars, including the British *Caprimulgus europaeus*; an allusion to their supposed sucking the udders of goats; hence also old English name 'goatsucker'.

211 Dartford warbler *Sylvia undata*; Sandwich tern *Sterna sandvicensis*.

212 They are the four known British breeding stations of the fork-tailed or Leach's petrel *Oceanodroma leucorrhoa*.

213 The (North Atlantic) gannet *Sula bassana*, so called from the Bass Rock, its oldest known colony.

214 To the increase in offal thrown overboard from fishing vessels of all kinds. But the possibility of a genetic mutation has also been suggested.

215 The two biggest colonies of avocets *Recurvirostra avosetta* in Britain.

216 First recorded breeding of snowy owl *Nyctaea scandiaca* in 1967.

217 In 1974; a pair had bred or attempted to breed since 1970 in the Lake District.

218 The white stork *Ciconia alba* on St Giles's, Edinburgh; the only known British breeding occurrence.

219 The great auk *Pinguinus impennis*. Last bird killed on St Kilda as a witch about 1840. (Last in world was killed at Eldey, Iceland, 1844.)

220 The goldcrest *Regulus regulus* or firecrest *Regulus ignicapillus*, now nesting in several English counties, are both about $3\frac{1}{2}''$ long and weigh $4\frac{1}{2}$ gms or about 0.16 oz.

United States Presidents

221 Four (1932, 1936, 1940, 1944).

222 1600 Pennsylvania Avenue, Washington, D.C.

223 Charles J. Guiteau, on 2 July 1881, at a railway station.

224 Abraham Lincoln.

225 Martin Van Buren.

226   Columbia University (New York City).

227   George Washington in his Farewell Address, 1796.

228   The Republican Party.

229   Grandfather and grandson.

230   Theodore Roosevelt, 1906, for negotiating peace in Russo-Japanese war. (Woodrow Wilson was awarded it in 1919.)

231   Abraham Lincoln.

232   James Buchanan.

233   The Speaker of the House of Representatives.

234   Andrew Jackson. (He lived at 'The Hermitage', a plantation near Nashville, in 1796. He returned there after his presidency and died there in 1845.)

235   William Howard Taft.

236   Philadelphia. (He was president 1797–1801. The government moved from Philadelphia to Washington during his administration. His son John *Quincy* Adams also became president.)

237   Theodore Roosevelt.

238   James K. Polk.

239   At least 35.

240   Thomas Jefferson.

General Knowledge 5

241   Well-preserved prehistoric cave paintings. (In the Dordogne Department of France, they have attracted millions of tourists and scientists from all over the world.)

242   A famous chef.

243   Infinity.

244   Two miles south of Wendover, Buckinghamshire.

245 Hungary.

246 Polo.

247 Karl Marx. (From the *German Ideology*, *XIth Thesis of Feuerbach*, written 1845, published by Engels in 1888.)

248 *The Good Soldier Svejk* (or Schweik).

249 Isles of Scilly. (On St Mary's Island.)

250 Hermes (a gift from him). (Hermes had stolen Apollo's cattle and it was a making-up gift; Hermes had invented it.)

251 Mine Workers union.

252 Claude Monet. ('Impression, Sunrise'.)

253 Ferdinand Magellan. (He was trying to find a route to the Spice Islands.)

254 President Sukarno.

255 'To a Mouse.'

256 The Battle of Jutland (31 May to 1 June 1916).

257 Sumo.

258 Jenny Lind.

259 $12\frac{1}{2}\%$ (one eighth).

260 Politbureau. (Its full name is Political Bureau of the Central Committee of the Communist Party. Called the Praesidium from 1952–66.)

The Works of J. R. R. Tolkien

261 Seven. (These are the rings of power listed in the verse epigraph to the *Lord of the Rings*.)

262 Oakenshield. (Thráin pronounced as dissyllable, Thra-in.)

263 Wormtongue.

264 Sharkey (also the Boss, but this is a title not a name
and so not an acceptable answer). (The Shire is the
country of the hobbits, laid waste by the wizard
Saruman near the end of *Lord of the Rings*.)

265 Bard (Bard the Bowman, Bard of Dale, or of Esgaroth
– but the name on its own is an acceptable answer).

266 He was the first hobbit to grow pipe-weed in the Shire.
(Pipe-weed might be tobacco, though the term is
not used by Tolkien: the phrase pipe-weed is a
necessary part of the answer.)

267 That of a bear. (He is a were-bear, in *The Hobbit*.)

268 Glamdring (this is Foe-hammer elsewhere, which is
just about acceptable: Beater, though, its goblin
nickname, is not acceptable).

269 Sméagol (this is the name used throughout the book,
but in the appendix Sméagol is said to be a
translation of Trahald: Trahald is therefore also
correct).

270 The Prancing Pony.

271 The Withywindle.

272 Elrond (he is sometimes called the Half-Elf, but that
is not his name, and not an acceptable answer).

273 Blotmath, pronounced Blodmath or Blommath.

274 Boromir (his brother Faramir received the same
advice, and is therefore acceptable as an answer, but
only Boromir acted on it).

275 A box of earth from her orchard, and the seed or nut
of a mallorn-tree.

276 The Ents. (These are also creatures of enormous size,
but benevolent and tree-like. Sauron the sorcerer
is said to have made the trolls during the Great
Darkness, as he made orcs in mockery of elves.)

277 Kingsfoil.

278 Snowmane, the horse of Theoden King of Rohan
(the second line of the epitaph is 'Lightfoot's foal,
swift Snowmane': but the name alone is sufficient
answer).

279 White horse on green field.

280 It is a worn-down form of 'hol-bytla', which means
hole-dweller (both the word and the translation
should be in the answer).

Grand Opera since Verdi

281 George Crabbe's *The Borough*.

282 It stopped at the point where Puccini had ceased
composing and Alfano had taken over – Toscanini,
who was conducting, laid down his baton and turned
to the audience saying, 'At this point the Maestro
laid down his pen'.

283 Strauss's *Intermezzo*, which describes an episode in his
early life and puts himself and his wife on the stage.

284 Prophetically, Wagner's *Götterdämmerung*.

285 An ape dressed in human clothing – Henze's opera
entitled *The Young Lord*.

286 Vrenchen and Sali, the lovers in Delius's opera,
A Village Romeo and Juliet.

287 Puccini's *La Rondine*.

288 W. H. Auden and Chester Kalman.

289 Krenek's *Jonny Spielt Auf* (the hero is a jazz-band
leader), produced at Leipzig in 1927.

290 The Viennese Waltz which had not been 'invented' as
a musical form at the time of Maria Theresa's Vienna.

291 Cardillac in Hindemith's opera of that name.

292 Arkel in Debussy's *Pelléas et Mélisande*.

293 Emily Marty (or just E.M.) in Janácek's *The
Makropoulos Case*.

294 *Julien.*

295 Wedekind's *Erdgeist* and *Pandora's Box.*

296 Poulenc's *Dialogue des Carmélites* which tells of the Carmelite Nuns going to the scaffold rather than renounce their beliefs.

297 Because the libretto was by Stephan Zweig who was Jewish.

298 *The Mother* by the Czech composer Alois Haba.

299 'Prima le parole; dopo la musica?' – what is more important in opera – words or music?

300 Shostakovich's *The Nose* in 1932.

General Knowledge 6

301 Desborough. (Now a nominal office, under the Chancellor of the Exchequer. Allows MPs to resign their seat.)

302 Analogue. (Transforms one quantity into another; the spring transforms weight into movement on a dial. Other types are digital or hybrid.)

303 René Descartes (1596–1650) in *Le Discours de la Méthode.*

304 Hoshea.

305 St Jerome (331–420). (The Vulgate is the Latin version of the Bible, and is still the authorised Latin version of the Roman Catholic Church.)

306 The Iona Community.

307 In Cape Town, to both Houses of the South African Parliament, on 3 February 1960.

308 The Maelstrom.

309 Little water.

310 Bombilla.

311 A newly married man – especially one who has long disdained marriage. (From the character Benedick in *Much Ado About Nothing* by Shakespeare. Benedick is also spelt Benedict.)

312 Anthony Trollope (1815–82).

313 Missouri.

314 A family of herbs, shrubs and trees. (Caper-spurge is one of the Euphoribiaceae; they have usually milky, often poisonous juice. Sometimes called the Mole Plant, as it is reputed to repel moles.)

315 Prince Henry of Portugal (1394–1460).

316 Athena tore up her work, Arachne then hanged herself and Athene turned her into a spider.

317 William Cobbett (1763–1835).

318 Clough Williams-Ellis. (A distinguished Welsh architect, his idea was to create a living museum of architecture based on Italianate styles.)

319 The Seychelles.

320 Sosigenes, an Egyptian astronomer.

The Old Testament

(References are drawn from the *New English Bible*, but other versions support.)

321 The fruit of the tree of knowledge of good and evil (Genesis 2.17).

322 Lice *or* Flies *or* Fleas *or* Maggots *or* Gnats (any of these will do) (Exodus 8.16–19).

323 Horeb, the mountain of God (Exodus 3.1).

324 Uriah (the Hittite) (II Samuel 11.1–21).

325 Adonijah (I Kings 1.5 ff).

326 Vashti (Esther 1.11 etc.).

327 Saul (I Samuel 28.7 ff.).

328 Anathoth (Jeremiah 1.1).

329 Ivory (I Kings 22.39).

330 Wash in the River Jordan seven times (II Kings 5.10).

331 Zedekiah (II Kings 25.1–7).

332 Eliphaz, Bildad, Zophar (Job 2.11).

333 *Either* Isaiah (2.4) *or* Micah (4.3).

334 The destruction of Nineveh (Nahum 1.1).

335 Lo-ruhamah (Hosea 1.6).

336 The threat of attack on Judah by the two kingdoms to the north, Ephraim (i.e. Israel) and Syria (or Aram, or the Aramaeans) (Isaiah 7.1–17).

337 In the second year of Darius, or 521 BC (Haggai 1.1 etc.).

338 A plague of locusts (Joel 1.1–7 etc.).

339 The fear of the Lord is wisdom and to turn from evil is understanding (Job 28.28).

340 YHWH or JHVH (Exodus 3.15).

The New Testament

341 'The time has come; the Kingdom of God is upon you; repent and believe the Gospel.' (Mark 1.15.)

342 Andrew and an unnamed disciple (John 1.35–40).

343 Deuteronomy (Matthew 4.4, 7, 10).

344 Zacharias and Elisabeth (Luke 1.5).

345 *Levi* in Mark 2.14 and Luke 5.27; *Matthew* in Matthew 9.9.

346 On her visit to Elisabeth, when the two women met and greeted one another (Luke 1.39–55).

347 Sosthenes (I Cor. 1.1).

348 Island of Patmos (Revelation 1.9).

349 Tertius (Rom. 16.22).

350 Philippi (Acts 16.12 ff.).

351 First and Second Letters of John ('One and Two John' is a correct answer) (I John 2.18, 2.22, 4.3, II John 7).

352 Talitha cumi, meaning 'Get up, little girl' or similar (Mark 5.41).

353 The Twelve Tribes (James 1.1).

354 Cyprus (Acts 15.36–39).

355 Tabernacles (John 7.2, 37).

356 Gentile Christians in Antioch, Syria and Cilicia. (Gentile Christians in Asia Minor is not a correct answer.) (Acts 15.23.)

357 A reference to 'Mark, my son' at the end of the First Letter of Peter (I Peter 5.13).

358 The edict of Claudius (Acts 18.2), the proconsulship of Gallio (Acts 18.12).

359 He circumcised Timothy (Acts 16.1–3).

360 (a) 2 (Acts 18.1 ff.; 20.2); (b) 3 (cf. II Cor. 12.14; 13.1).

General Knowledge 7

361 Mercury.

362 The Portland Vase.

363 Montreal.

364 Flea (human flea).

365 James Bridie (1888–1951).

366 Stanley Baldwin. (Abdication in 1936.)

367 Wombat.

368 Access to the Baltic. (The corridor was 10 miles wide and 100 miles long, and contained the port of Danzig.)

369 King Henry IV. (In *King Henry IV Part I* by Shakespeare.)

370 Stoning them to death.

371 The Russo-Japanese War of 1904–5. (The Portsmouth here is that in New Hampshire, USA. President Theodore Roosevelt mediated.)

372 Generally the concealment of one heavenly body by another passing between it and the observer. (Also the disappearance of a star in the sun's rays when in apparent position near that of the sun. The concealment of a heavenly body behind the earth's body.)

373 Alhambra.

374 Oliver Cromwell.

375 Rio de Janeiro.

376 Battle of Tel-el-Kebir (13 September 1882).

377 The Harp of Ireland.

378 Emily Post (née Price).

379 Twelve gold stars on an azure blue background.

380 The Hall of Arts and Sciences. (Opened under this name by Queen Victoria on 29 March 1871.)

The Works of Dorothy L. Sayers

381 'As my Whimsy takes me.'

382 Paul Austin Delagardie, his uncle.

383 The Marlborough and the Egotists.

384 Robert Eustace (*The Documents in the Case*).

385 Sir Impey Biggs (*Strong Poison*).

386 He kept canaries (*Strong Poison*).

387   The Warden of her College (*Busman's Honeymoon*).

388   She got a £250 cheque for the Latymer scholarship
      (*Busman's Honeymoon*).

389   Twenty years (*Busman's Honeymoon*).

390   A manuscript letter of John Donne (*Busman's
      Honeymoon*).

391   Detective Inspector Parker (*Clouds of Witness*).

392   Château Yquem (*Clouds of Witness*).

393   The Soviet Club (*Clouds of Witness*).

394   110a Piccadilly (*Clouds of Witness*).

395   *Unnatural Death.*

396   Dr Penberthy. He shoots himself. (*Unpleasantness
      at the Bellona Club.*)

397   A new prosodic theory of verse (*Gaudy Night*).

398   It was burnt (*Gaudy Night* – not scrawled on or
      defaced).

399   Elizabeth Drake, in *The Documents in the Case.*

400   As 'a synthetic preparation in racemic form'
      (*The Documents in the Case*).

Norse Mythology

401   Mjollnir (Myol-neer).

402   Heimdall(ur) (Haym-dall(er)).

403   Hoth(ur); he threw the mistletoe twig that killed
      Baldur.

404   Freyja (Fray-ya).

405   The antler of a hart.

406   The rowan (mountain ash).

407   Othin's gold bracelet from which eight bracelets of
      equal weight dripped every ninth night.

408 Sleipnir (Slaypneer) had eight legs and Starkath(ur) was born with eight arms.

409 Prosperous voyaging; good fishing; wealth in lands and goods.

410 The mead of poetry.

411 The nails of dead people; Loki (Lokk-i) in one source, Hrym(ur) in another.

412 He kicked him into the fire at Baldur's cremation.

413 Othin, who is said to have learnt secrets of the dead by communing with victims on gallows.

414 He changed himself into a hawk and Ithunn into a nut and flew off with her in his talons.

415 Hel had Baldur.

416 The giant Hrungnir in combat with Thor stood on his shield because he had been falsely warned that Thor would attack him from underground.

417 Runes (probably representing occult secrets in general).

418 A separate goddess whom Frigg set to protect people she wished to keep from danger.

419 Baldur appears as a just and innocent victim; Balderus appears as lustful and pugnacious.

420 The use of the verb 'help'; a trinity of divine figures; the idea of an omnipotent god.

General Knowledge 8

421 Karl Heinrich Marx (in 1843).

422 St Omer.

423 The Boer War.

424 Seven young men and seven maidens for the diet of the Minotaur.

425 (a) Verbatim, (b) Literatim.

426 Four (*Das Rheingold; Die Walküre; Siegfried; Götterdämmerung*).

427 Nostradamus (1503–66), the Latinised name of Michel de Notre Dame.

428 Aurora.

429 Barnes Wallis.

430 Spanish, French, American.

431 Hecuba.

432 Colonel (Draga) Mihailovic. (Chetniks were the Serbian Resistance movement. Britain eventually backed the other, more effective Resistance movement – the Partisans – led by Tito.)

433 Jackal.

434 Carl Jung (1875–1961).

435 By the sparrow. Erithacus rubecula is the zoological name for the robin. (The zoological name for the sparrow is Passer. Passer domesticus = house sparrow: Passer montanus = tree sparrow.)

436 The highest part of the withers (which start at the base of the crestline of the neck).

437 Pop art cartoons.

438 Edward VII (1901–10).

439 Albert Einstein.

440 Pope Alexander VI (Rodrigo Borgia).

Railways of Great Britain

441 2–8–2.

442 Central, St Enoch, Buchanan, Queen Street.

443 No. 92220 ('Evening Star').

444 6000.

445 100A1.

446 Colchester, 1981 ft. (Formerly Manchester Victoria/
Exchange, not now extant.)

447 Calling-on arm permitting a train to pass a stop
signal at danger.

448 630V DC.

449 A GWR bogie ventilated van.

450 Waterloo and City (SR); Mersey Railway (LMR).

451 Sir Herbert Walker.

452 GWR route via Slough, Addison Road and the West
London Extension Railway.

453 Bowness (Lake Windermere).

454 3200 hp.

455 Taff Vale.

456 Restaurant/Kitchen/Buffet Car.

457 119, Class T9.

458 Cromford and High Peak line.

459 New Street (Snow Hill being now closed).

460 Thursoe.

British Chemical Industry

461 Mrs Margaret Thatcher.

462 Monomers. (Single molecules is an alternative
answer.)

463 As a detergent (products such as washing-up liquids).

464 Shell and ICI.

465 In lubricating oil purification.

466 Dichloro-Diphenyl-Trichloroethane.

467 Acetone.

468 They stand for 'American Selling Price' (a method of assessing for duty imports of chemicals into the USA).

469 Terms applied to residual gases after liquefaction in the process of manufacturing liquid chlorine.

470 J. R. Whinfield (a research chemist working at Calico Printers Association Ltd).

471 Manufacturing polyester fibres. ('Terylene', although a trade-name, would be acceptable.)

472 Nitrogen, phosphorus and potassium.

473 Organic sulphur compounds (the word mercaptans is also acceptable).

474 2-naphthylamine can cause papilloma of the bladder (cancer) or (alternatively) 2-naphthylamine is a carcinogen.

475 The air- or gas-filled space above a liquid in a closed container.

476 Air.

477 Methyl ethyl ketone (79.6° C.). Ethyl alcohol has boiling point 78.5° C.

478 The name for the residue after a batch distillation.

479 Ammonia and carbon dioxide.

480 Acetylene.

General Knowledge 9

481 Francis Bacon (of studies).

482 Tutsi (also known as Watutsi, Batutsi or Watussi, herdsmen of Rwanda and Burundi, Central Africa).

483 On the Queen's birthday (21 April).

484 On a twin-lens camera. (This has two lenses, one above the other, one being a viewing and the other a taking lens. They have widely different views of a subject, necessitating parallax compensation.)

485 Baron Manfred von Richthofen, German airman of World War I.

486 Zeus. (Mnemosyne was their mother.)

487 Henry IV.

488 Dido. (Virgil makes her fall in love with Aeneas.)

489 Meissen.

490 Hephaestus, god of fire and metal-working. (Hephaestus made her, the other gods gave her a variety of wicked traits.)

491 Martin Luther King.

492 Figures of horses carved on slopes of chalk hills (Westbury, Wiltshire; Uffington, Berkshire).

493 Pike.

494 San Sebastian.

495 Dash-dash-dash.

496 Sisyphus.

497 Sandwich Islands. (Discovered in 1778 and named after the 4th Earl of Sandwich.)

498 'I', says the Quarterly,
So savage and Tartarly;
'Twas one of my feats.'

499 Jan van Eyck.

500 Medusa.

Famous Russians

501 Ivan IV (the Terrible).

502 Peter I.

503 Kropótkin.

504 Stanislávsky.

505 Lénin.

506 A. Lunachársky.

507 Scriábin.

508 P. D. Uspensky.

509 Mikhail Fédorovich.

510 Lomonósov.

511 Mikhail Shólokhov.

512 Pugachev.

513 Sumarókov.

514 Vassily Kandínsky.

515 Rublev.

516 Hérzen.

517 Yesénin.

518 Blok.

519 A. V. Samsónov.

520 Nikoláy Lobachévsky.

Geography of Great Britain

521 Bare, flat limestone surfaces between furrows or fissures.

522 Snowdon (more strictly Y Wyddfa, at 3560 feet the highest of Snowdon's five peaks).

523 West Lancashire, between the estuaries of the Ribble and the Wyre (or the area of which Blackpool is the chief town).

524 A mass of hard sandstone found particularly in southern England on the chalk downs.

525 York.

526 A seasonal or intermittent stream which flows in chalk country after heavy rain.

527 Mean sea level measured at Newlyn, Cornwall.

528 Peak District.

529 From: Shetland, Orkney, Caithness, Sutherland, Ross & Cromarty, Inverness, Argyll.

530 It formed a natural defensive line for Hadrian's Wall.

531 All are nuclear power-stations.

532 Central Business District.

533 A strong north or north-east wind blowing downhill from Cross Fell (or any strong wind blowing downhill in the northern Pennines).

534 Ardnamurchan (point or peninsula).

535 NE to SW alignment of mountains and faults (or the grain of the country).

536 A hard rock sometimes used for building, from the Lower Greensand in Kent (or the Hythe Beds of the Lower Greensand).

537 Nothing, or a flock of sheep or a Land Rover, etc. (the 'Roads' are former shorelines of a lake which fluctuated in level because of damming by ice at different heights).

538 The Forestry Commission.

539 Institute of British Geographers.

540 Transverse Mercator.

General Knowledge 10

541   Masada. (Masada was a great rock on the edge of the
Judaean desert where the Zealots made their last
stand against the Romans. When defeat was certain
their leader persuaded them to draw lots to select
10 men to kill the remaining 960 defenders. One of
these finally slew his nine fellows and then slew
himself.)

542   The capybara of South America.

543   Eagle (as a heraldic symbol).

544   The Royal Pavilion, Brighton. (Designed for the
Prince Regent by John Nash in the style of an Indian
Emperor's palace complete with onion-domes
and minarets.)

545   Queen Charlotte, wife of George III.

546   Cosmo Gordon Lang. (Lang, a Scotsman, was born
in 1864 and died in 1945. He was Archbishop of
Canterbury from 1928 until his retirement in 1942,
when he was created Baron Lang of Lambeth.)

547   7 November. (This is, of course, the Russian October
Revolution, 1917.)

548   Rome.

549   Pound. (In divisions of 100 Agorot.)

550   Henry VI (1440).

551   His flight around the Eiffel Tower in an airship.

552   French Foreign Legion.

553   The first Cambridge College (Peterhouse). (Hugh
de Balsham was the Bishop.)

554   On the Panama Canal.

555   London University in 1878.

556   Joseph Stalin.

557   The Atlantic Charter. (A statement of principles.)

558 Local Government.

559 Epsom salts.

560 A charm (or chirm).

English Literature

561 John Masefield (in 'Sea Fever').

562 The Venerable Bede.

563 Metaphysical Poets.

564 William Shakespeare (Sonnet LXXI).

565 A. E. Housman.

566 Translation of Homer (Keats's 'On First Looking into Chapman's Homer').

567 Aran Islands, Ireland.

568 *Grace Abounding*.

569 Gerard Manley Hopkins (first published in 1918).

570 Richard Lovelace.

571 Robert Burns.

572 The execution of King Charles I.

573 The French King Louis XI.

574 John Locke.

575 His sister Mary, in a fit of insanity, stabbed her mother to death and wounded her father.

576 Christina Rossetti.

577 Thomas Hobbes (*Leviathan, the Matter, Form and Power of a Commonwealth, Ecclesiastical and Civil*).

578 It has no name.

579 Wilkie Collins.

580 *Frankenstein*.

History of Music

581 *Third* or *Eroica.*

582 One (harpsichord).

583 Johann Christian (youngest son of Johann Sebastian).

584 Musician or violinist.

585 Frederick the Great.

586 Lélio (by Hector Berlioz).

587 Marcellina.

588 Schumann.

589 *Oberon.*

590 Mannheim (by Charles Burney, in 1772).

591 *Don Giovanni* (supper scene).

592 Peter.

593 Dr Thomas Arne.

594 Green (in *Die böse Farbe*).

595 Wellington's (at Vittoria) entitled *Wellington's Victory.*

596 Handel composed the *Utrecht Te Deum* and *Jubilate* for the celebration of the Peace of Utrecht in 1713, by which England kept Gibraltar.

597 'Hamlet' Funeral March (volley-firing behind the scenes).

598 Vivaldi.

599 Beethoven's *Mass in D* or *Missa Solemnis.*

600 La ci darem (from *Don Giovanni*).

General Knowledge 11

601 Medmenham (near Marlow on the River Thames).
(The Hell Fire Club was a notorious 18th-century
côterie founded about 1755 by Sir Francis Dashwood,
afterwards Baron Le Despencer. Its 13 members
conducted their profanities and revelries at
Medmenham Abbey, which formed part of the
Dashwood property.)

602 Benjamin Disraeli, Earl of Beaconsfield.

603 After the second Battle of Philippi. (Marcus Junius
Brutus (c. 86–42 BC) was successful against Antony
and Octavian in the first Battle of Philippi, though
Cassius was defeated.)

604 (The) highest town (or city at the top). (From the
Greek akros = highest, polis = city.)

605 Arms limitation (Strategic Arms Limitation Talks).

606 Strophe, antistrophe and epode.

607 Herculaneum.

608 Lord Clifford's (Walter de Clifford). (Mistress of
Henry II and poisoned by Queen Eleanor in 1177.)

609 Laputa.

610 For bravery in the field. (The MM was instituted by
George V in 1916.)

611 Ten.

612 Peace. (Eirene was the Greek goddess of peace.)

613 Animals of the open sea, far from any shore, such as
the jelly-fish, the whale sharks, whales, young
herring and a great variety of small crustaceans.
(Living or growing at or near the surface of
the oceans.)

614 Isle of Sheppey.

615 The Julian Calendar was then introduced. (46 BC had 455 days. The Julian Calendar was based on a solar cycle of 365¼ days, but this was superseded by the Gregorian calendar which rectified the overplus of a few minutes each year, and was adopted in England in 1752.)

616 Award for bravery in support of law and order. (Awarded by the Goldsmiths Company in memory of Capt. Ralph Binney who stopped a robbery in 1944. Applies only to the City of London and cannot be awarded to a policeman.)

617 Sir Thomas Lawrence. (The correct title is 'Master Anesby'.)

618 Théodore Simon.

619 Epsilon.

620 Patricide and incest. (He murdered his father, Laius, and married his mother Jocasta.)

Personalities in Russian History and the Arts

621 The Selected Council.

622 It was abolished by Peter the Great.

623 It lasted from 1598 to 1613. During these years there were five Tsars in Moscow, all of whose claims were doubtful. The period ended with the establishment of the House of Romanov.

624 Ingria in Sweden.

625 A law whereby each monarch was to nominate his own successor.

626 A statesman who rose from a poor Moscow family to be Peter the Great's most powerful collaborator in his reforms.

627 To dislodge the British from India.

628 Archpriest Avvakum.

629 The abolition of serfdom and the establishment of a liberal constitution.

630 On that very day he had signed a decree approving a plan for a representative assembly.

631 Konstantin Petrovich Pobedonostsev, Procurator of the Holy Synod.

632 Yekaterina Breshko-Breshkovskaya, the 'grandmother of the Russian Revolution'.

633 *Eugene Onegin* and *The Queen of Spades*.

634 *Letter to Gogol* (from Belinsky).

635 Pavel Petrovich Kirsanov.

636 Gorky (the other two were Tolstoy and Chekhov).

637 *The Idiot*.

638 Chekhov. (Tolstoy refused to resign because he did not recognise the existence of the Academy.)

639 Ivan Bunin.

640 Tolstoy's. (Rumour spread in the West that the writer was dead some days before he actually died.)

English Cathedrals

641 Bishop Robert Poole (he instituted the work in 1220 and it took 45 years to complete).

642 The nave and aisles of St Paul's cathedral which, from the fifteenth to the nineteenth century, were used for the sale of goods and as a promenade for the citizens of London.

643 Peterborough.

644 Lincoln.

645 Winchester.

646 Gilbert Scott.

647 Worcester Cathedral.

648 To the signing of Magna Carta (1215) when the royal power was curbed by the barons.

649 Gloucester.

650 The cathedral of Christ Church, Oxford.

651 The Benedictine order.

652 It was used by the monks to watch over the treasures in the shrine of the patron saint.

653 Bristol.

654 Southwark.

655 The north-west transept.

656 Chester (half-way along the north side of the nave).

657 Exeter (Bishop Oldham's Chantry, 1519 – the owls being a punning reference to the founder's name).

658 Behind the high (or main) altar (thus preserving the plan of the sanctuary normal till *c.* 1000).

659 John Piper.

660 In the cloisters of Gloucester Cathedral.

General Knowledge 12

661 Estonia (now a Russian Republic).

662 Len Murray (at the Annual Congress in September 1973).

663 Thomas Aquinas.

664 Howard family (Dukes of Norfolk).

665 Pietro Badoglio.

666 15th Century. (This collection of letters, preserved by the Pastons of Norfolk, was written between *c.* 1420 and 1503. They give a unique picture of domestic and political life.)

667 *Morning Post.*

668 Isle of Avalon.

669 The Phoenix Park murders.

670 Sir Edwin Henry Landseer.

671 Iowa.

672 Caspian Sea.

673 Avoca (County Wicklow).

674 Democritus.

675 Abu Dhabi.

676 Leah.

677 Glubb Pasha (Sir John Bagot Glubb).

678 *Love's Labour's Lost.*

679 André le Nôtre.

680 Mrs Patrick Campbell.

British Church Architecture

681 13th Century (early English).

682 The tower of St Botolph's Church, Boston, Lincolnshire (built 1409–50).

683 A compartment off a main room, especially off the nave of a Saxon Church; also called an *exedra* or *oriel*, in some cases.

684 James Gibbs.

685 Durham Cathedral, sanctuary and chancel aisles (built 1093–1104).

686 Sompting, Sussex.

687 Chichester.

688 Royal hall.

689 Henry Yevele (pronounced Yeaveley).

690 The carved leaves of its decorated capitals.

691 Ely.

692 Brian Thomas.

693 John F. Bentley (1839–1902).

694 St Andrew, Roker by E. S. Prior (built 1906–7).

695 A junction of mouldings at right angles in which the joint is horizontal instead of at 45°.

696 Hexham. (Its 1300th anniversary was in 1974.)

697 Churches built for the commissioners appointed to administer the Act of 1818 providing a million pounds for building new churches. (There was also a commission of 1715 but the term is usually applied to churches under the 1818 Act. There were about 230 of them.)

698 The spire of St Mary's R.C. Cathedral was designed by J. A. Hansom who invented the 'Patent Safety Cab' named after him.

699 Henry Flitcroft (built 1731–3).

700 A stone lintel with an arch-shape cut out of it, as in the Saxon part of St Peter's, Bywell.

Grand Opera

701 It was a theatre built on land that had once belonged to the church – a Convent Garden – given at the time of the dissolution of the monasteries by Henry VIII to the Duke of Bedford.

702 *King Lear.*

703 Franco Alfano.

704 The name by which the Paris Opéra (or Académie de Musique) was affectionately known. Verdi especially refers to it as such in his correspondence.

705 On the Viennese critic Eduard Hanslick, who disliked Wagner's music. Wagner originally was going to call the character Hans Lick.

706 Literally the Italian for realism. The term used to describe the realistic or naturalistic school of Italian opera as typified by Mascagni, Leoncavallo, Giordano and Puccini.

707 It began with *Siegfried*, so that the great German tenor Max Alvary could make his London début in his favourite role.

708 In Cilea's opera, *Adriana Lecouvreur*, in which the character is called Michonet.

709 They are all tenors; they are all Spanish characters; and they are all loved by a Leonora.

710 Leonard Warren, the American baritone, who collapsed during a performance of *La Forza del Destino*; the tenor Aroldo Lindi who collapsed and died in San Francisco during a performance of *Pagliacci*.

711 Opéra comique is the French term for operas with spoken dialogue, generally a light subject, though this is not a necessity; Opéra-Comique is the name of a theatre in Paris, originally the home for French musical pieces with spoken dialogue.

712 Rossini's *The Barber of Seville*.

713 Arrigo Boito.

714 Richard Strauss's *Die Schweigsame Frau* (The Silent Woman).

715 *Oberto, Conte di San Bonifacio* (1839).

716 They are all heard off-stage before they make their entrance.

717 In Mozart's *Marriage of Figaro*, Figaro and Marcellina use the words *I Masnadieri* (The Robbers) in Act 3.

718 Maria Callas and Joan Sutherland respectively.

719 She sings a piece by the French composer Grétry.

720 Walther von der Vogelweide (or the Birds) according to Walther, in his song to the Masters.

General Knowledge 13

721 The Dunkirk evacuation plan (26 May – 4 June 1940).

722 Henry II or Richard I or John. (The early Plantagenet kings from Henry II to John. Henry II (1154–1189) was the son of Matilda (daughter of Henry I) and Geoffrey Plantagenet, Count of Anjou. John lost Anjou in 1204.)

723 Moslem (Islamic, Muslim or Mohammedan). (The year began 25 January 1974 and contained 354 days – year 1395 began 14 January 1975.)

724 Holland. (The Royal Dutch Airline KLM was established in 1919 and flew a passenger service between Amsterdam and London from May 1920. A holding company of SAS, the Danske Luftfartelskab, was founded even earlier, in 1918, but their scheduled service ran only between August 1920 and 1946.)

725 *La Boutique Fantasque*. (Choreography Massine; music Rossini; arranged Respighi.)

726 Clement Attlee.

727 Bishop James Ussher. (It was accepted as the basis of Biblical chronology into the early 20th century. He was Archbishop of Armagh.)

728 John Bunyan.

729 Leucippus. (5th century BC. It was elaborated by his pupil Democritus.)

730 Casquets Lighthouse (or Caskets).

731 Chess – he held the title for 28 years.

732 A calf. (Used especially in cheesemaking, rennet occurs naturally in the stomach lining of calves. Rennet is also used to make junkets. It can also be a type of apple or a farrier's tool.)

733 D. W. Griffith.

734 Zug.

735 *Béatrice et Bénédict.* (Berlioz wrote the libretto himself – the opera was first produced in Baden-Baden in 1862.)

736 Francis Drake's *Golden Hind.* or *Pelican.*

737 Ballistic Missile Early Warning System.

738 1848 (often called 'the year of revolutions').

739 Island of Staffa (Inner Hebrides).

740 Orang-outang.

History of World Theatre

741 Aristophanes (the only comic writer: the others all wrote tragedies).

742 Christopher Marlowe and Johann Wolfgang von Goethe.

743 Henrik Ibsen, the Norwegian dramatist.

744 John Heminge and Henry Condell.

745 Henry Fielding (it was, of course, only abolished in 1968).

746 *The Playboy of the Western World.*

747 Antonin Artaud.

748 Kurt Weill.

749 Jean-Louis Barrault.

750 John Gay's *The Beggar's Opera* (staged by the theatre manager John Rich in 1728).

751 The American playwright Clifford Odets (not to be confused with *Waiting for Godot* by Samuel Beckett).

752 The Shaw Theatre (Euston Road).

753 Sir John Gielgud.

754 The Living Theatre.

755 Chester, Wakefield (or Townley), York, Coventry.

756 The Theatres Royal, Drury Lane and Covent Garden ('theoretically', because there were many ways in which the monopoly could be evaded).

757 Tommy Steele.

758 George Devine.

759 Eduardo and Peppino.

760 Joseph Grimaldi.

19th-Century English History

761 Corrupt Practices Act, 1883.

762 Lord Palmerston (1865).

763 Don Pacifico.

764 £20,000 a year.

765 Lord Cardwell.

766 Free sale; Fair rent; Fixity of tenure.

767 7d in the £ on incomes over £150 per annum.

768 Cowper-Temple. (Under the terms of the 1870 Education Act the clause proposed by W. F. Cowper-Temple granted this right.)

769 Grand Old Man; Murderer of Gordon (Gladstone).

770 Richard Cross (Disraeli was Prime Minister).

771 It listed financial abuses of the Church of England, pluralities, stipends, etc.

772 Samuel Smiles.

773 The Duke of Cambridge.

774 The City of London.

775 Lord Palmerston.

776 Supervision of registration of electors.

777 Attendance at places of worship.

778 H. Rider Haggard.

779 Sir John Seeley, 1883.

780 The Electric Telegraph Company – for use and control of their services.

The Iliad and the Odyssey

781 Eumaeus, the swineherd.

782 Ilium is a name for Troy. The Iliad is the Trojan (poem).

783 Nestor.

784 Priam.

785 A scar left by a boar's tusks.

786 The wrath of Achilles.

787 Poseidon did his utmost to prevent Odysseus' return home.

788 That of a landless labourer or *thes*.

789 As vultures sitting on a tree: *Iliad VII*, 59.

790 Glaucus: *Iliad VI*, 146.

791 Astyanax, son of Hector.

792 Pandarus.

793 Odysseus and Telemachus on being reunited.

794 Ares, god of war.

795 Xanthus.

796 A sea horse having two forefeet and a body that ends in the tail of a dolphin or fish.

797 Milman Parry.

798 Well before 1200 BC. Representations date from the 15th and 16th centuries BC.

799 After 750 BC, 750–675 acceptable.

800 Iris.

General Knowledge 14

801 He was the Regent of Hungary.

802 Thomas Henry Huxley.

803 Tara (County Meath).

804 The mho (ohm spelt backwards).

805 Simone de Beauvoir. (She won the Goncourt prize in 1954.)

806 Execution of Admiral Byng.

807 Martha. (By Edward Allbee.)

808 Castor and Pollux.

809 Agrippa (M. Vipsanius Agrippa). (Later rebuilt by Hadrian.)

810 English (Robert Malthus, 1766–1834).

811 Pounded almonds and sugar.

812 Goonhilly Downs, Cornwall. (Although the television communication was the most dramatic aspect of the work at Goonhilly, the GPO's main concern was with radio-telephone communications.)

813 Gerard Manley Hopkins (1844–89).

814 *Pilgrim's Progress* (written by John Bunyan in 1675).

815 There was a riot after two drawn games between Celtic and Rangers.

816 After King Sisyphus in Greek legend who was condemned to roll a huge rock eternally uphill but when it reached the top it fell back.

817 Elektra (or Electra).

818 New Zealand (it is the NZ portion of Antarctica).

819 Konrad Lorenz. (Translated from the German by Marjorie Kerr Wilson.)

820 Otto Rank.

Classical Mythology

821 Saturday (Saturn).

822 Poseidon.

823 Polyphemus.

824 Tyre.

825 A tree nymph.

826 The Phaeacians or Phaeaces.

827 Ajax.

828 Calliope.

829 Cadmus.

830 Children of the primeval marriage of heaven and earth.

831 Theogony.

832 Hyacinthus.

833 Thyestes.

834 Amphiaraus.

835 Virgo.

836 Psyche.

837 Arachne.

838 Zeus.

839 She forced Zeus to appear in his true shape.

840 Artemis.

Arthurian Literature

841 Sir Bedwere, or Bedivere (in the French *Vulgate* it is Sir Girflet).

842 Sir Bors, Sir Percival, Sir Galahad.

843 Igrayne, duchess of Cornwall (other versions have Ygaerne and Igerne).

844 Mons Badonicus, or Mount Badon.

845 Emperor, or Procurator, of Rome allegedly killed by Arthur.

846 The twelfth.

847 The sixth.

848 Sir Balin (or Balain).

849 Sir Bertilak (or Bercilak) de Hautdesert.

850 Speak to him unless addressed.

851 Lancelot had killed his brothers Gareth and Gaheris (or, in the *Vulgate*, his brother Gaheriet).

852 An adder. (A knight drew his sword to kill it, so that both sides suspected treachery.)

853 Mordred was the son of Arthur and Morgawse, Arthur's half-sister. The relationship was therefore both father and son, and uncle and nephew.

854 Sir Mellyagaunce (or Meleagant, or Meliagrance).

855 Ron.

856 The Welsh *Gododdin*.

857 King Pellinore's.

858 To stand by the mad goshawk Cully, till the bells ring three times.

859 It belonged to the Fair Maid of Astolat, Elayne le Blanke.

860 He is 'a blooming boy' in knight's armour.

General Knowledge 15

861 *The Origin of Species*. (On the Origin of Species by means of Natural Selection, or the Preservation of Favoured Races in the Struggle for Life.)

862 Uncle Remus.

863 Harry S. Truman.

864 Nitrogen.

865 Rorschach.

866 Cuckoo.

867 The Devil.

868 Grendel.

869 56.

870 Brezhnev and Kosygin.

871 Caustic soda or caustic potash or lye.

872 Scheherazade, by telling him a story (*The Arabian Nights*) each night.

873 Laser.

874 Henry Moore.

875 He was thrown through a window.

876 Mountains or hills.

877 Republic of South Africa.

878 Winston S. Churchill.

879 Dr Samuel Johnson.

880 Ergotism.

Kings and Queens of England

881 James II.

882 Henry V.

883 Her 'Golden Speech'.

884 Emperor Henry V and Geoffrey of Anjou.

885 William Rufus.

886 Yea-and-Nay (Oc e No – meant he kept his word).

887 Fontevrault (in France).

888 A blank sheet of paper with a royal signature.

889 George V.

890 Francis I of France (Field of the Cloth of Gold).

891 Lucy Walter.

892 Porphyria, a disturbance of the porphyrin metabolism – the process producing pigments in the blood.

893 Housing.

894 Her grandmother had been Henry VIII's sister (and Mary Tudor had been declared illegitimate by Henry).

895 Her nickname for John Whitgift, her last Archbishop of Canterbury.

896 When Princess Beatrice was 21 (in 1878) at Osborne.

897 Queen Anne.

898 He would give them Buckingham Palace.

899 Born 'in the purple', when the father was king.

900 John.

Shakespeare's Plays

901   Rosalind (*As You Like It* I, iii, 127).

902   Edgar as Poor Tom (*King Lear*, III, iv, 118).

903   *Timon of Athens*.

904   Petruchio (*The Taming of the Shrew*, IV, i, 93).

905   Of Queen Gertrude, his mother (*Hamlet*, I, ii, 146).

906   *All's Well that Ends Well* (spoken by the Countess of Rousillon).

907   Falstaff (*Henry V*, II, iii, 15).

908   'Britain shall be fortunate, and flourish in peace and plenty' (V, v, 442).

909   Lead (*The Merchant of Venice*, II, vii, 15).

910   Baptista, a rich gentleman of Padua (*The Taming of the Shrew*).

911   Vienna (*Measure for Measure*, IV, i).

912   Bottom (by Titania in *A Midsummer Night's Dream*, IV, i, 36).

913   *Two Gentlemen of Verona* (IV, ii, 40).

914   Yorick (*Hamlet*, V, i, 202).

915   Dogberry (*Much Ado About Nothing*, IV, ii, 88–93).

916   Figs (*Antony and Cleopatra*, V, ii, 234).

917   Hamlet (*Hamlet*, V, ii, 371).

918   Don Adriano de Armado (so described in the dramatis personae of *Love's Labour's Lost*).

919   The crown of the King of England (*Henry IV Pt 2*, IV, v, 22).

920   A simple constable.

Other BBC Quiz Books

Mastermind

This first *Mastermind* book is still available containing selected quizzes from the popular BBC1 'brain game'. There are questions on a wide range of specialised subjects – politics, aeronautics, antiques, gardening – and many general knowledge questions.

Ask the Family

A quiz book with over 500 questions and answers from the BBC tv series to test the family's general knowledge and provide plenty of enjoyment.

Ask the Family: 2

Another selection of brain-teasers from the popular BBC1 quiz programme, with hundreds of questions and answers for those who want to play the game at home or test their general knowledge.

Brain of Britain
John P. Wynn

Hundreds of questions and answers from Radio 4's long-running general knowledge quiz game. There are sections on sport, music, history and literature, and quiz enthusiasts will be able to test themselves or organise a family quiz.

Round Britain Quiz

A selection of over 400 questions and answers from the popular Radio 4 quiz programme, which combines the ingenuity of the crossword with erudition and wit.